DUNSTABLE
WITH THE PRIORY
1100 – 1550

Vivienne Evans

This book is the first volume of a trilogy on the History of Dunstable since 1100. Later volumes are to cover the periods 1550 to 1850 and 1850 to the present day.

First published October 1994
by
The Book Castle
12 Church Street
Dunstable
Bedfordshire LU5 4RU

ISBN 1 871199 56 5

Cover: Conjectural drawing by Bernard West of the early 15th century Gate House archway (back) and the outside of the Prior's Lodging (front) of Dunstable Priory. By courtesy of Dunstable Town Council.

Computer typeset by Keyword, Aldbury, Herts.
Printed in Great Britain by the Alden Press, Oxford.

ABOUT THE AUTHOR

Vivienne Evans is one of Bedfordshire's most experienced history lecturers and authors. In addition to leading dozens of local history courses, she has also written numerous books and booklets including History All Around; John Bunyan, his life and times; Folk, characters and events in the History of Bedfordshire and Northamptonshire; The Dunstable Swan Jewel; Chronicle featuring Middle Row; The Book of Dunstable and Houghton Regis; and Falkes de Breauté and the Siege of Bedford Castle. She also runs a tourism and research organisation called Dunstable Historic and Heritage Studies.

AUTHOR'S ACKNOWLEDGEMENTS

During the Autumn of 1980 my friends, Joyce Maxfield and Barbara Hull, and myself worked at Barbara's kitchen table and with a great deal of help from Laura Enscoe, who typed out the original manuscript, Omer Roucoux and John Bailey, who produced the maps and pictures and Mike Snoxell, who at that time was manager of Prontaprint – Luton, we produced the small paperback booklet 'A Brief History of Dunstable with the Priory'. At the launch in December, we had the pleasure of welcoming Paul Bowes, who had recently opened The Book Castle, in Church Street, Dunstable.

Since then I have had continued help and encouragement from a great number of people, especially from Barry Stephenson of the Special Local Collection at Bedford Reference Library, the staff at the County Record Office, County Hall, the Rector, staff and congregation at the Priory Church of St. Peter, Richard Walden and members of Dunstable Town Council and the hundreds of Dunstablians who attend my lectures, town walks and outings.

This time it has been Marlene Pothecary and my daughter Rosamond who have had to wrestle with my writing and my husband Lou who has had to put together the illustrations and I thank them all. However, without our friend and publisher, Paul Bowes, whose patience, encouragement and help at every stage have made this book possible, we would not have been able to share with the people of Dunstable a little more information about the important history of our town – and we are extremely grateful to him.

CREDITS TO PICTURES

AJC	Alan Clark
DTC	Dunstable Town Council
MD	Produced for Moore's of Dunstable by Countryside Arts
RD	Roderick Davies
LPE	Lewis Evans
FAF	Alec Fowler
JH	Jim Hayes
AL	Andrew Leech
JL	John Lunn
BM	British Museum
OR	Omer Roucoux
MS	Marquess of Salisbury

I would like to thank the above for permission to use their drawings and photographs. In particular Dunstable Town Council for the use of the drawings which they recently commissioned from Bernard West.

The Gregorian Calendar

When using dates it must be remembered that in 1752 there was a major change in the British system of recording them. Up until then the 'year' had begun on March 25th, but when Britain adopted the Gregorian Calendar it began on January 1st. This sometimes leads to apparent inaccuracies. Where possible the dates in this book have been adapted to the New Style of recording.

CONTENTS

INTRODUCTION

In Roman times, an important settlement, known as Durocobrivis, had been established at the crossroads of two of the most famous roads in England – Watling Street and the Icknield Way – but for centuries before the Norman Conquest the site had been deserted. However, soon after 1100 the advisors of King Henry I saw the advantages of re-establishing a 'new town' there on the royal estate of Houghton.

Following a personal invitation from the King, businessmen were attracted from a wide area to take up building plots along three of the main roads, the fourth, East Street, Henry kept for himself. On one side a palace was built, which soon became known as Kingsbury. On the other side Henry gave land to a group of Augustinian Canons, who built a priory.

The first recorded royal visit was when Henry and his court stayed at Kingsbury in 1109. From then on, nearly every king and queen of England stayed in Dunstable. When Kingsbury became too expensive to maintain, they stayed at the Prior's house and after the Dissolution and the closing of the Priory, at the White Horse Inn.

Royal patronage brought wealth to the Priory and the town. The latter grew very rapidly and became an important centre for the marketing of wool, grain and leather; travel was also and important industry.

The Priory hostel, still standing in High Street South, provided accommodation for the numerous travellers passing through the town. Somewhere on the other side of the road was the almonry for poor travellers and up on, what is now, Half Moon Hill stood the Leper Hospital.

Probably the best known royal visit was in 1290, when King Edward I led the funeral procession of his late queen, Eleanor, into the town. Some years later an 'Eleanor' cross was built on the crossroads to commemorate the event.

Henry VIII and his first wife, Catherine of Aragon, were frequent visitors to the town but the best known royal event which took place in the town, was the conference, in 1533, which arranged the annulment of their marriage. Catherine had made her last visit but Henry continued to come, as did his children and some of his later queens.

Apart from the recorded royal visits and those of church and government leaders the people of Dunstable must have been used to seeing great processions of richly dressed horses and riders coming into the town and commandeering all the best accommodation. Long before 1500 there were far too many travellers, pilgrims and tourists for them all to find beds at the Priory. Inns, such as the Saracen's Head in South Street, opened on both sides of the crossroads.

Although travellers brought income to the town and created numerous jobs they were not always welcome. Unemployed and homeless families drifted into the town looking for work; some such travellers brought disease, others fell on hard times and became professional beggars. Medieval soldiers were often kept waiting for their pay and supplies; on more than one occasion the people of Dunstable were robbed and the buildings damaged by soldiers passing through the town. It may have been when Queen Margaret of Anjou passed through the town with an army that a solid gold brooch, the emblem of the Swan Knights, was deposited or lost at the Dominican Friary. It is now called the 'Dunstable Swan Jewel' and is in the British Museum.

However the town prospered and in the 15th century there were enough wealthy residents to found a fraternity, dedicated to St. John the Baptist. They paid for their own priest to serve at an altar in the Priory Church. Elaborately decorated pages from their register are in Luton Museum and an extremely beautiful and valuable funeral pall, bought by one of their members, is in the Victoria and Albert Museum.

Although at times the Priory had a 'cash flow' problem it was a house of high repute. The prior was usually a man respected both within his own Order and within the wider church. Many of the canons were also educated men. They have left us three sets of documents (all published) which give us a great deal of knowledge about their business affairs and the control they wielded over the townspeople, and the villages where they owned land and churches. Unfortunately we know very little about their day-to-day lives but by consulting reports from other Augustinian houses we can learn a little about the work of the different officers. Providing hospitality and care to travellers must have been an important part of their work and the medieval text book, written by Dr John Gaddesden, of Little Gaddesden, during the 14th century, points out to us the type of medical care that the infirmarian would have offered to sick and weary travellers.

Henry III invited followers of St. Dominic to settle in South Street, opposite the Priory; they were very popular in the town and the canons were jealous. Their friary was never a big house and was closed early on in Henry VIII's scheme for dissoluton. The friars received no pensions and we cannot tell what happened to them but across the road, Prior Gervase Markham had time to find positions for many of his canons.

He surrendered the Priory at the end of December, 1539 and retired, with a generous pension, to a house in High Street South. The canons received much smaller pensions and gradually found jobs, as clergymen, in various parish churches. Like the majority of the religious houses most of the Priory buildings were taken down. However, the people of Dunstable had for centuries maintained their end of the Priory Church, so were allowed to keep it as their parish church. Today visitors from all over the world visit this much loved 'Priory Church of St. Peter'.

For a few years the rest of the buildings were spared, while plans were discussed to convert Dunstable Priory into a cathedral. However the money slipped away and the scheme was abandoned. The hostel, Priory House, was sold as a private house but the rest of the buildings were taken down. Stones, robbed by the local people for repairing their buildings can still be seen around the town.

Far from going into a decline Dunstable prospered, as houses and unprofitable warehouses were converted into inns.

Even more travellers passed through the town and in addition to accommodation for people and horses men found work as blacksmiths, wheelwrights, and saddlers while the ladies began their own branch of the tourist industry by making souvenirs, especially hats, from locally grown straw.

Chapter 1

Dunstable Before The Priory

The Villages Around The Crossroads

Excavations by the Manshead Archaeological Society of Dunstable in 1964 proved that the Roman town of Durocobrivis lies under the modern town of Dunstable. Durocobrivis was, however, deserted during the early fifth century, at a time when unpaid Saxon mercenaries wandered the roads making it unsafe to live in unwalled towns. It is probable that some of the residents moved away to the west of England whilst others went to live on the surrounding hills. Soon after, Saxon immigrants, mercenaries and the native Romano-British fought across this area and, as the buildings crumbled, weeds, shrubs and eventually small trees grew over them.

The Anglo Saxon Chronicles record that in 571AD the army of Cuthwulf took Limbury and passed on down the Icknield Way, leaving this area a safe place for Saxon immigrants to settle. The roads were still dangerous, however, and these farmers avoided the crossroads, choosing sites under or near the present Houghton (Regis), Sewell, Caddington and Kensworth.

During the tenth century the raiding parties and armies of the Danes ravaged the countryside and the roads were again particularly unsafe, but in 1017 the Danish King Canute united the Saxons and the Danes, and the local villages began to prosper. At some unknown date, most of South Bedfordshire became the king's own demesne land – meaning land which was farmed to produce food for the royal household. Caddington was given to a nobleman called Edwin who built a house on the top of Blows Downs, possibly near Zouches Farm, overlooking the Watling Street and Icknield Way. Later Edith, wife of Edward the Confessor, separated Sewell from Houghton and gave it to her 'man' [servant] Walraven.

The land of Sewell was north of the Icknield Way (Tring Road – West Street) across to the west side of Watling Street (High Street North – Chalk Cutting); Houghton land was east of Watling Street, across the Icknield Way (Church Street – Luton Road area including Jeans Way) to Blows Downs and along the bottom of the Downs to Watling Street; the plateau on Blows Downs across to (modern) Markyate was Caddington,

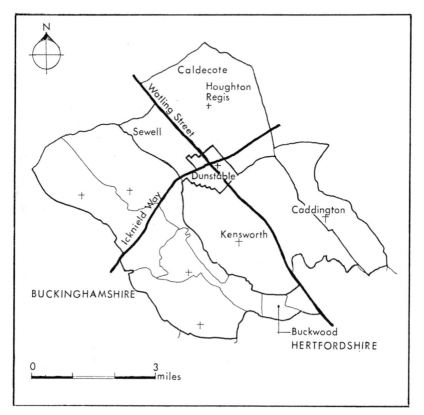

The land of Dunstable taken from Houghton Regis and Kensworth, also marking Buckwood.

and the land west of Watling Street across the Dunstable Downs to the Icknield Way belonged to Kensworth (see map).

Around the crossroads, excavations have uncovered Roman ditches, wells and masonry, therefore the area probably remained uncultivated.

The Evidence For the Name 'Dunstable'

The name used for the new town in the twelfth century was Dune/staple (or Dunstapel) – two Saxon words, meaning 'Downs' and 'Standing Post'; a name to signify either where the land of these four communities met near the Downs, or perhaps where the Icknield Way crossed the Watling Street. The site-name probably pre-dates both Henry I and the Norman Conquest. The important fact is that the king owned all four corners of the crossroads.

The Village of Caddington

About the year 1053, Edwin of Caddington made his will, dividing his property between St. Albans Abbey and his son Leofwin[1]. Caddington was mainly a forest of mature trees, with a community at the present village and possibly other settlements in the clearings. The county border divided the plateau. Leofwin made Caddington into two separate manors (estates) and gave one (The Bedfordshire Luton side) to St. Paul's in London and kept the remainder, near Dunstable, for himself.

The Coming of William of Normandy

No more is heard of Leofwin after the Battle of Hastings, unless he is the 'Leofwin' who held approximately 180 acres at Boarscroft, near Tring, both before and after 1066. [Domesday Book Herts.] William the 'Conqueror' led his army around London to Berkhamsted, where the church and secular leaders invited him to London to become the next king. 'Nevertheless, in the meantime they harried everywhere they came'[2].

---

1   Bedfordshire Historical Record Society [B.H.R.S.] Vol. V. (This is not Earl Leofwin, brother of King Harold but may be some relation.)

2   Anglo Saxon Chronicles [A.S.C.] 1066.

The soldiers lived off the land but officials claimed the demesne land of Edward the Confessor in the name of the future King William and these estates were left unharmed. From the values given in the Domesday Survey, Houghton, Sewell, Kensworth and Leofwin's (Dunstable) end of Caddington were considered 'royal' and unharmed. St. Paul's claimed their end of Caddington by 'the King's writ' and as a result the soldiers were allowed to take what they wanted (as they did in most villages round here) and the value of the manor fell from £5 down to ten shillings (50p) per year.

When William became king, he gave Kensworth and the Dunstable side of Caddington to St. Pauls who developed a large farm (possibly near Zouches) for which an inventory of 1299 survives[1].

The Evidence Of The Domesday Survey
William rewarded the noblemen who had contributed to his victory with gifts of land scattered across the country. They shared their land with their relatives and senior officers, who installed ex-soldiers and others as tenants.

Once England was reasonably peaceful, William and his officials devised the great tax survey. The figures show, if we leave out the admitted towns of Bedford, Berkhamsted and St. Albans, that Houghton had the highest population of any community with the same acreage in this district; and more per acre than either of the king's market towns of Luton or Leighton. Twelve of these Houghton residents were not classed as villagers, (agricultural labourers), but as small-holders who had some craft with which to support their families.

The travelling clerks who collected information for the survey had a list of questions nearly as rigid as our present tax forms. There was no 'column' for anything a little out of the ordinary. I personally think that several of the Houghton 'small-holders' were trading at the (Dunstable) crossroads. They were not free burgesses (businessmen), nor were they all

---

1   B.H.R.S . Vol. 1.

BEDEFORDSCIRE

Houstone dñicũ cõ regis. p̃ x. hiđ se defđ. Tra e
.xxii. cař. In dñio .ii. cař 7 uilli .xxii. cař. Ibi xxx
7 vii. uilli 7 xii. borđ. p̃ai .xii. cař. Silua .c. porc.
Inð coai redđ p ann .x. lib ad pensũ. 7 dimid die
de frumto 7 melle 7 aliis reb, ad firmã regis panemab.
De minutas csuetudinib 7 de .i. fumario. lxv. fot.
De csuetud canu. lxv. bt. 7 Regine .ii. unc auri.
De cremto qđ misit suo caIlebosc. iii. lib ad pensũ xx
fot de illo argento. 7 i. unc auri uicecomra.
Ecctam hui cõ ten Wills camerari cu dim hida.
que ad eu pan 7 de .x. hid manqu e. Tra e dim cař.
7 ibi eft. Valet .xii. fot pannu.
Sewelle p .iii. hid se defd T.R.E. Tra e .ii. car. Ibi eft
.i. car 7 dim. 7 adhuc dim por fieri. p̃ai .iiii. bou.
Ibi .i. uilts 7 iiii. bord. trija ual 7 ualure .xx. fot. Hanc
tenuit Walraue ho eddid regine. 7 potuit dare cui
uoluit. In odeqoft hund iacuit T.R.E. Radulf u
caIlebosc in cõ houstone eam appofur ccedente .W. rege
p cremtu qd ei de lit. hoc dñm hoef eid Rað. fed in
jđ cu dicqe audig. ~~Actha huno~~

The Houghton Regis entry from Domesday Book.

5

the land and their landlord in the feudal way. They were neither villagers with a large amount of arable land with which to support their families, nor landless serfs. So the only column under which to put them was 'small-holder' which basically they were, as trading was probably a sideline.

Another fact uncovered by the Domesday survey, is that the royal manor of Houghton had a church, with about 60 acres of land for its support. The only other recorded churches in Bedfordshire were in the county town of Bedford and the royal towns of Leighton and Luton. Why then was it necessary to have one at Houghton?

The Evidence for the Names 'Houghton' and 'Regis'

Luton, Leighton and several other local places were also royal manors, yet Worthington Smith[1] refers to the Saxon word 'saelig' or fortunate in connection with Houghton; medieval documents refer to King's Houghton. William [the king's] Chamberlain – who owned the land of Luton Church (600 acres approximately), Houghton Church (60 acres approximately) and several other pieces of land – when witnessing the documents of Henry I, chose to call himself 'William de Houctone'[2]. Why was Houghton especially fortunate or royal?

The Obituary of William I

The monks wrote '. . . Among other things we must not forget the good order he kept on the land, so that a man of any substance could travel unmolested throughout the country with his bosom full of gold . . .'[3] In other words, it was safe once more for travellers and traders to use the roads.

---

1   W.G.Smith [W.G.S.] Dunstable, its History and Surroundings.

2   An example can be found in 'An Outline Itinerary, Henry I' 1134 by W. Farrer.

3   A.S.C .1086.

Chapter 2

Henry I Founds Dunstable
– Around 1100

William I died in 1086 and his son William II lost much of his inherited wealth fighting his brother Robert Duke of Normandy. England was greatly neglected and law and order deteriorated.

William's younger son Henry came to the throne in 1100 and promised to 'abolish all the injustices which were prevalent during his brother's reign'. The war with Robert continued and Henry was seldom in England, nevertheless '. . . no man dared to wrong another. He made peace for man and beast'[1].

During the twelfth century various land owners tried to improve their revenue by developing their rural manors into market towns. Instead of the low profits of agriculture, which fluctuated with the weather, they would get the reliable returns of cash rents for houses, shops and market stalls and a 'tax' on business done in the market. If the landowner was the king, he would also get higher personal taxes and possibly a tax on pack-ponies, imports and exports, but to have a market it was necessary to have a wide road; the Watling Street was ideal.

Whether or not the people of King's Houghton were already living and trading around the crossroads, sometime soon after 1100 the financial advisers of Henry I decided to develop Dunestaple as a market town.

---

1   A.S.C. 1100.

The King's Palace – Kingsbury

The Victoria County History quotes an old document printed in Dugdale's Monasticon Anglicanum, in which it is said Henry encouraged settlers by promising them land at an annual rent of 12d. (5p) an acre and the privileges accorded the burgesses of London and that he 'built there a Palace called Kingsbury'[1].

So Henry had a 'palace' built on the land of Houghton. Again, we have no exact date but the Totternhoe stone was cut, dried and carted, the carpenters and others did their work, and the palace was furnished and staffed ready for King Henry I and his party of courtiers to stay there in 1109[2].

It is entered in the Pipe Rolls that he paid a steward or housekeeper 1d. per day to look after the palace in his absence. This was never a royal residence but a sizeable house where royal parties could stay while they were travelling. At times these were very large parties and included noblemen and senior church officers, each with their own party of retainers. In 1122 and in 1131 Henry held his Christmas court at Kingsbury when people from all over England would have travelled here to see him. The visit in 1109 was probably his first visit to Dunstable and it is possible that he received petitions and complaints concerning the running of his new town. While he was here in Dunstable, he signed a document which gave royal authority for his Queen, Matilda, to adapt Holy Trinity Aldgate (London) into a House of Augustinian Canons[3].

The villagers and smallholders of Houghton were mainly feudal tenants, completely under the thumb of the king's steward and unable to educate their sons or to travel without his permission. The men who settled in Dunstable were burgesses (businessmen) who had no such feudal ties and there was no lord of the manor to administer the town in the king's name. These burgesses might not have accepted the rule of a steward and the town was too small to support trade guilds, or a mayor and council.

Sitting here in Dunstable, signing the deed about the

1   Victoria County History [V.C.H.] Vol. III, p.356.
2&3 W. Farrer, An Outline Itinerary, Henry I.

foundation of Holy Trinity, did he consider bringing canons to Dunstable? Some years later it was one of the Holy Trinity founders who brought a party of canons to found the Dunstable Priory. Henry certainly admired their work and personally sponsored several more houses. They were educated men who were not in an enclosed order and who here in Dunstable would provide a church, a school and a manor court, organise the running of the town and as a bonus they could provide accommodation for travellers.

The Augustinian Priory

In the tenth and eleventh centuries, groups of clergy shared a communal house and walked or rode around the villages. Most of Bedfordshire was visited by canons from St. Paul's, Bedford[1]. The parochial system as we know it only became generally established in the late twelfth and early thirteenth centuries. These early priests were called canons. At the very end of the eleventh century the canons of St. Botolph, Colchester, decided they would like to copy some French houses and follow the 'rule' of St. Augustine, based on a letter he sent to some nuns at Hippo. One of their number was a Norman, familiar with the French 'Augustinians', and he had described them. He and another brother, Bernard, were chosen to go to France to see how the system worked in practise. They travelled for some time and about 1105 returned and helped adapt St. Botolph's to the new rule to become 'Canons Regular'. Then in 1107 'Norman' and Bernard were released and led a group of brethren to start Holy Trinity Aldgate, sponsored by Queen Matilda[2].

The papers and records of Holy Trinity have survived and record that some years later Bernard led a group to start a house at Dunstable. Unfortunately, they do not give a date. The original surveyors, building supervisors, lay brothers, masons and other craftsmen, must have arrived some years before the main party.

---

1   H. Cobbe. Luton Church, p.356.
2   J.C.Dickinson. The Origins of The Austin Canons.

Excavation by the M.A.S. of original Friary oven and replacement bee-hive ovens. A.J.C.

From the excavations carried out by Manshead Archaeological Society on the site of the Dominican Friary, to the
south-west of the crossroads, we know that in this case the first
settlers dug sleeper trenches in the chalk, wedged in tree
trunks, cut holes in them, placed uprights in the holes and from
this frame they made simple wooden accommodation. At a
later date, the wooden walls were replaced by permanent walls
of Totternhoe stone. Also, the first cooking hearth was a
fireproof floor of tiles on edge, but later it was replaced by
beehive ovens.

The same would have happened at the Priory; the workers
living in wooden huts worshipping in a wooden church whilst
the stone buildings were constructed. J. C. Dickinson[1] stressed
the unreliability of charter dates when assessing the start of a
religious building; we do know that by 1130 there were enough
canons settled in the new buildings for Henry to issue a general
notification that he had granted the manor of Dunstable to his
'nascent monastry of Dunstable'[2].

King Henry I Gives Dunstable To The Priory
The charter was issued about 1131 '. . . know ye that I for God
and my health and the souls of William my son and Matilda the
Queen my wife have given to the Church of the Blessed Peter of
Dunstable which I have founded in honour of God and of the
same Apostle and to the Canons Regular there serving God in
perpetual and free alms, the whole Manor and Burgh of
Dunstable with the lands of the same vill . . .'[3].

Then he goes on to describe the details: the land, the market
and the schools. Keeping for himself his own houses and
garden he gave the Priory the valuable gift of the Totternhoe
stone quarry and the right to use the common pasture of
Houghton, Caddington and Kensworth, with a share of the
wood of Houghton. Then came the legal details which gave the

---

1   J.C.Dickinson. Monastic Life in Medieval England.
2   W.Farrer. Notification addressed generally of the grant to the 'nascent
     Monastery of Dunstable . . . of the Manor of Dunstable'.
3   V.C.H. Vol. III, p.316.

Prior very wide powers over the people of the town and ending with '. . . as much liberty as Royal power is able to confer.'

Events in the Early History of Dunstable
There are several pieces of information which have contributed to our knowledge of the early years of Dunstable, although it is sometimes hard to separate fact from legend. Here are their sources:

Dunn the Robber
The 'Treatise of Dunstable', written at the Priory between 1280 and 1290 includes the story of the robber called Dunn, who terrorised the neighbourhood and gave his name to the town 'Dun's stable'[1]. This has given credence to the story and shows that it was already circulating before 1300. The story of 'Dunn the Robber' was used when the Victorian 'Arms of Dunstable' was designed: a post or 'staple' with a ring fastened to it by a staple. According to W. H. Derbyshire it was drawn about 1840[2]. He published a ballad about Dunn in his book.

> The King put a poull (post)
> '. . . In that roade-highway, where so many passe,
> And in the Poull let drive a staple strong,
> Where to the Kinge's owne ringe appendant, was,'

The story goes on that Henry challenged Dunn to steal the ring and although soldiers and others kept watch, the ring was gone in the morning and Dunn had got safely away. The implication of the story being that this caused Henry to clear the trees and, by building the town, free the area from robbers. A curate called John Willis in 1600 used the legend to decorate the frontispiece of the first Dunstable Parish Register; this also seemed to make the story more official. Worthington Smith gives several versions of the story.

---

1   B.H.R.S. Vol. IXX.
2   W.H.Derbyshire. A History of Dunstable.
     Blaydes. Notes and Queries, Vol. I.

The School of Geoffrey de Gorham

This true story is entered amongst Thomas Walsingham's account of the lives of some of the abbots of St. Albans. Unfortunately, he did not date events, only the years that each abbacy started and ended[1].

Abbot Richard of Albini 1097–1119 wanted a master for the Abbey School. Sometime (unstated) after the post had been filled, Geoffrey de Gorham, a notable scholar from Caen arrived. He stayed 'sometime' with Abbot Albini, who then suggested he should start a school in nearby Dunestaple. As only the sons of 'free' men could attend school, there must have been a large settlement of burgesses there well before 1119.

The boys enrolled, the school was started and time passed. Coming from France where such things were more common, de Gorham attempted to put on a play. It was based on the life of St. Catherine of Alexandria who rejected the God Mars in favour of Jesus Christ. She was martyred on the knives of a revolving wheel, from which our Catherine Wheel fireworks get their name.

His actors were probably his pupils and he borrowed for them the copes, sometimes translated as choristers' robes, from St. Albans Abbey; they were probably embroidered with gold and silver. Then tragedy struck; de Gorham's house caught fire and the copes were destroyed. This attempt may have been the earliest miracle play performed in this country, so perhaps the fire was arson by some person enraged by the thought of what he saw as sacrilege? Anyway, de Gorham lost the valuable copes belonging to St. Albans! He left his school and entered the Abbey as a 'penitential' monk.

All this must have taken place early in the reign of Albini, because de Gorham progressed, won the confidence of his fellow monks, and was elected the next Abbot in 1119.

---

1   Records of the Abbey Chroniclers. Published in the Rolls Series.

Henry's Visit of 1122

The entry in the Anglo Saxon Chronicles for 1123, which includes Christmas 1122, records 'In this year the King spent Christmas at Dunstable, and messengers from the Count of Anjou visited him there'. This is the first time the Chronicles record Henry at Dunstable and it has led some people to think it was his first visit. The reference to the messengers of the Count of Anjou is interesting. There was a great disaster in 1120 when 'The White Ship' sank on a journey back from Normandy. Prince William, (Henry's heir), his other legitimate son and many others were drowned. The young widow of Prince William was the daughter of the Count of Anjou. She returned home but Henry did not return her dowry; the 'messengers' were seeking the dowry and Henry feasted and entertained them here in Dunstable. His chancellor, Ranulf, invited the party to visit Berkhamsted Castle. On January 1st the whole noisy and still celebrating party rode up West Street and across the downs. When they were in sight of the castle, they quickened their pace and suddenly Ranulf fell from his horse. They were going too fast to stop and one or more horses went over him. So the celebrations came to an abrupt end. The royal party remained at Berkhamsted until January 10th, when they moved on to Woodstock. There Henry became involved in matters of state and the messengers returned to Anjou empty handed.

Chapter 3

The Roles of Canons Within
An Augustinian Priory

The Augustinian canons were a working order who at times carried out duties outside the Priory but they normally returned each evening. They had lay brothers (see Charter 274 below) who may have lived in a hostel adjacent to the Great Court and they also had secular workers.

The Role of the Prior[1]
He was the most senior official and father of the house. Richard de Morins was the fourth prior and the first of which we know any details. He was already a well known and respected scholar when he arrived in Dunstable from Merton Priory in Surrey. During his long period as prior from his arrival in 1202 until his death forty years later, he studied in France and travelled in England, representing both the Pope and the head of the Augustinian Order. He entertained Royal parties, archbishops, bishops and many important visitors, was responsible for the writing of the Annals and for bringing the respected relic, the bones of St. Fremund[2] to Dunstable. His work and reputation brought an increasing number of visitors and pilgrims to the Priory and increased the prosperity of both the Priory and the town.

---

1   For the duties of various officials within an Augustinian house of canons
     see: John Willis Clark, The Observations in Use in the Augustinian Priory
     of St. Giles and St. Andrews in Cambridgeshire, 1897.
2   The life of St. Fremund, a reputed son of King Offa, is now considered to
     be confused by legend.

All the priors had to be capable of entertaining royal visitors and discussing national affairs. They were also called upon to act as official messengers for the king, the pope and the Archbishop of Canterbury and to visit other monasteries and priories to give advice and make reports. At home they were responsible for the well being and discipline of their House and for the careful and sympathetic selection of other officers. Many matters concerning the House were discussed at the daily meetings in the Chapter House and often two or three senior canons were consulted before a decision was made, but the final responsibility was the prior's. De Morins, who was so often away from the Priory, would have had an assistant and these absences may have been part of the reason for the very bad relationship between the town and the Priory in the early 13th century.

Later Priors Have Problems. Dunstable Priory quickly grew to become one of the more important Augustinian houses. It was very well endowed but like all concerns where the income was mainly dependent on agriculture, income fluctuated with the weather and the price of wool and corn. This together with the frequent royal visits and responsibilities for the care of all poor and sick travellers along the two main roads, meant that at times they were very poor indeed. This is why Prior Richard de Morins fought so hard for the Priory's privileges (see below). When he died, in 1242, after forty years in office the Priory was prosperous and respected. The very first winter of his successor, Geoffrey of Barton, Priory-owned sheep died on the hills of Derbyshire and the seed corn rotted in the fields of Bedfordshire. Starving people, not only local but also from a great distance, squatted along the streets of the town. He managed to struggle from year to year but when around 1260 there was another long spell of cold wet weather, which spread from one winter to the next, he was probably glad to retire. In 1262, when he handed over the responsibility to Simon of Eaton, the Priory was in debt. They had borrowed from Henry Chadde, one of the wool exporters, and in addition they had sold their next year's wool in advance. One summer, as they waited anxiously for the next harvest, the canons had to give up bread from their own table to keep the horses fed!

Between 1242 when Richard de Morins died in 1351 there were six priors, one of whom was deposed and four of whom resigned.

The Next Two Priors Share 122 Years! Then in 1351 Prior Thomas Marshall was elected and remained in office for 62 years. He was followed by Prior John Roxton who continued for another 60 years, resigning in 1473. Between them they guided the Priory through the second half of the reign of Edward III, the 22 years of his grandson Richard II, the three Lancastrian Kings, into the Wars of the Roses and halfway through the reign of King Edward IV, (of York). Roxton was followed by three more priors about whom we know little, but during the early 15th century, in common with the majority of religious houses, the Priory declined.

Although even more travellers stopped in Dunstable, many of them used the inns rather than the Priory hostel. The Fraternity (see below) had taken on an important religious and social role within the town. However, not only did less young men come forward to become novices but also benefactors were more likely to make gifts to the new educational establishments, to the fraternities and even to the friaries rather than to the traditional monasteries and priories. Luckily for the canons, the last Prior, Gervase Markham, elected in 1525, was a most clever and astute man and smoothly arranged the closing of his house, having found positions for many of the canons and suitable accommodation for himself.

The Priors of Dunstable
This is the list of priors, together with their dates, researched and published by Worthington G. Smith. Most of his information came from the Annals of the Priory and as he points out the spelling is not always reliable.

PRIORS

Bernard, dates not known.

Cuthbert, dates not known.

Thomas, occurs 1185, resigned 1202.

Richard de Morins, elected 1202, died 1242.

Geoffrey of Barton, elected 1242, resigned 1262.

Simon of Eaton, elected 1262, died 1274.

William le Breton, elected 1274, deposed 1280.

William de Wederhore, elected 1280, resigned 1302[1].

John of London, elected 1341, resigned 1348.

Roger of Gravenhurst, elected 1348, resigned 1351.

Thomas Marshall, elected 1351, resigned 1413.

John Roxton, elected 1413, resigned 1473.

Thomas Gylys, elected 1473, resigned 1482.

Richard Charnock, elected 1482, resigned 1500.

John Wastell, elected 1500, died 1525.

Gervase Markham, elected 1525, surrendered 1540.

The Cellarer

He was the canon who was in charge of organising the finances
of the Priory. He had the overall responsibility for the houses
that they owned in Dunstable and all the farms, houses and
churches in the surrounding villages. This made up most of
their income. On the other hand he was responsible for the
purchase of food, drink, clothes and fuel and for the overall
running of the bakehouse, brewhouse and kitchen. One of the
matters to which he had to give much thought was the
provision of the store rooms; the dried and salted fish, the
bacon, wine, salt and such spices as they could afford for
special occasions. He was often away from the Priory,
inspecting their property, checking on the progress of crops,
harvesting and threshing and also making quite sure that their
representative was strict in collecting all the tithes. Unlike in a
secular manor, he and his assistants worked as both indoor and
outdoor stewards.

---

1   Despite help from the registrar of the Lincoln Cathedral records,
Worthington Smith was unable to fill the gap between 1302 and 1341.

The Kitchener

This was the canon who took over responsibility from the cellarer once supplies arrived in the store rooms. He had to be prepared to arrange elaborate meals for the important parties and to find a way of providing a healthy diet for the canons when the pantry and store rooms were nearly empty. In addition to the preparation of the food he also had to make sure that the cooking and serving vessels were clean and unchipped and that the tables were correctly and suitably laid.

The Infirmarian

This canon was in charge of the infirmary and the sick and elderly canons. In every community there were elderly brothers who were allowed to withdraw from the strict routine of the priory and its very austere diet. They had no other home than the priory and were allowed to live their remaining years in more comfortable conditions and with food which was more suitable to their lack of teeth and ageing digestive systems.

He may have gone out into the town to treat the burgesses

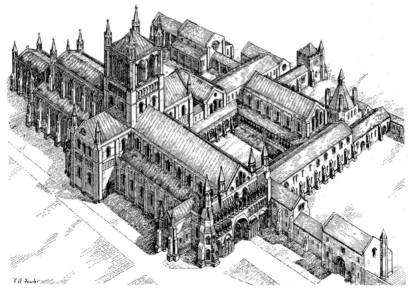

Conjectural picture of the buildings which made up the Augustinian Priory. F.A.F.

and their families but the poor people of Dunstable and especially the vagrants and poor travellers would have been treated by the almoner.

The Almoner and The Hosteller

Although both of these officials offered hospitality on behalf of the Priory their work was quite different. John Willis Clark recorded:

'**The Almoner** should be kind, compassionate, godfearing, discreet and careful. He must look after pilgrims, beggars and lepers that came to his house and in the town and he must visit the old, lame, bedridden and blind. His job was to clothe, feed and comfort but he must not receive those who are sick without first asking the Prior.

The Hosteller must be a suitable choice to converse with all manner of guests of both sexes, so he must be well brought up. "He is that by which the house is judged." He must supply food and drink as required, clean cloths, towels, cups and silver spoons, mattresses, sheets, blankets, pillows, quilts, a clean bowl for washing, a candle and a good fire.'

The Sacristan

From a list of duties prepared at Barnwell Priory, in Cambridgeshire, we learn that he had to make the church 'useful and in every way seemly'. In practice this meant that he was responsible for the safety, the cleanliness and complete care of the inside of the church and its contents. He also had to see that all the lights were cleaned and kept burning on the altar and before the statutes. Richard and Ralph Young (see below) were among several burgesses who gave the sacristan 'lights' or wax to burn before the altar or statues. Not only did he have to buy wax for the better quality candles used in the church but also mutton fat and tallow for the inferior candles used in many parts of the domestic and working rooms in the Priory. His duties also included ringing the church bells.

The Novice Master

This was another responsible position, which involved the

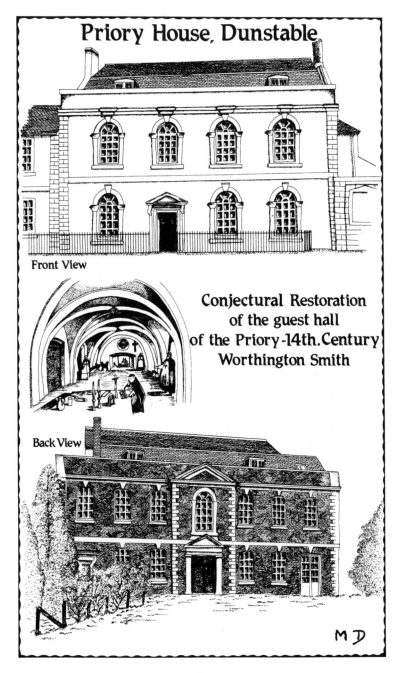

Priory House, Dunstable

Front View

Conjectural Restoration of the guest hall of the Priory-14th. Century
Worthington Smith

Back View

MD

training and disciplining of new entrants. He trained them to take part in the strict routine of their house and all the different services and helped them to overcome any feelings of homesickness or reluctance to give up their previous worldly life. While he was supervising their general and religious education, he had to keep a constant watch to make sure they were suitable to fit into the strict Augustinian routine of prayer, worship and work. Not only to make sure that they had a genuine religious vocation but also that they were physically strong enough to live a life where, although bedtime followed a short service at 8.00 p.m., their sleep was broken at around 2.00 a.m. for the first of six church services and they had to be up ready to start their day with the second service at 6.00 a.m.!

The Precentor

Sometimes this job was shared with a Librarian, but in Dunstable he was probably responsible for all the books at the Priory and also the music. He chose special settings for the different services and also led the singing and made sure everybody was issued with the correct music. The novice master would have relied on the precentor to train the novices to take part in the choral part of the services[1].

Lay Workers

When the Priory closed there was only the prior, sub prior and eleven canons so they must have relied heavily on secular, paid officials. Even in the 14th and 15th centuries there were probably no more than 20–25 canons. In earlier centuries some of the unskilled work would have been carried out by lay brothers; men of less education and from a lower social background than the canons.

From the Charters and Treatise we can find some interesting details of the early appointments. Numbers ( ) are taken from B.H.R.S. X.

---

1   John of Dunstable (c.1370–1435), a respected musician at the court of Henry V, was educated at St. John's College, Cambridge, but may have previously been a choir boy at the Priory. Music that he composed is in the Bodleian Library, Oxford, and in several European collections.

(274) A Lay Brother. Among these may have been Adam le Mon' of Maulden. He became a lay brother about 1202. His terms of reference were, that '. . . so long as he wear the dress of the laity, it shall be to him in bread and drink and of general commons (extras) that we make provision for lay brothers . . . both bread and beer and also of the broken meats of our house as lay brethren are used to be given . . . in addition we give him clothing, each year five shillings . . . and if he shall be infirm, or will not be able to do full work because of weakness, we shall do to him those alms as are due to our household servants, both in life and in death . . .' In return, Adam was to 'swear those faiths and dilligences to us . . . and to our house and our business wherever the same may be . . .'

(276) A Gaoler. Before 1202 Adam of Upton entered the Priory service as a janitor. He was to take charge of the prisoners in the prison '. . . in a sufficient and competent place'.

Derbyshire[1] claimed that the prison stood in the centre of the town, under Middle Row, (now number 23 High Street South); he described one cell extending under Back Street and another under the High Street. This was more likely to have been a cold store than a prison, because the Annals record that the prison was pulled down and rebuilt in 1295 which suggests that it was a separate building. Middle Row was still workshops and market stalls in 1202 (see below).

Adam was to 'have provisions, and stipends and usual fees'. He and his wife and family were to 'restrain from diminishing the Prior and also the Priory'. His servant was to do only the Prior's work and not the business of the janitor. If he or his servant should breach any of the terms of the agreement, Adam would pay the Prior ten shillings.

(299) The Secular Priests
The Priory soon owned many of the local churches. They took the profit of the church land and the tithes and sent one of their

---

1   W.H.Derbyshire. The History of Dunstable. p.156.

canons out to take the services. The Lateran Council of 1215 condemned this practice; Bishop Wells of the Lincoln Diocese insisted they should appoint resident vicars and many of our local vicarages began in 1200 or soon after. These resident vicars were known as secular priests.

About 1210, the Priory appointed Geoffrey of Woodford as curate and master clerk. While '. . . he shall live in church of Dunstable, he will receive each week 4 loaves of white bread of the best kind of the canons, another 4 loaves of the second kind and in any day a gallon of beer of the free servants . . .' He was also to have soup and a serving from the main dish of the day. 'Thus if the servants are served meat one of the best portions is kept for him' also fish. If eggs were shared out, he was to get five. He was to get four shillings per year as stipend but he must not lay claim to offerings.

(748) The Prior must have delayed appointing fully-qualified priests, because it was 1225 before he announced that he had appointed two secular priests and that Alexander Young, who owned the windmill and other property in West Street, was to pay thirty-four shillings each year for the maintenance of the second priest, in return for which the superior priest should make daily prayer for the souls of Alexander and his family.

The Priory Treatise gives more details of the two priests. They had a house and an attendant to look after them. They were allowed straw twice a year to renew their beds. They had a deacon to assist them who also had his main meal provided by the Priory kitchens. He was given no bread but the parishioners were instructed to make him a gift of sheaves each autumn! He had no regular stipend but was allowed ¼d. out of every 6d. [put in the collecting boxes], and up to 1d. out of every two shillings, but no more. Out of his meagre income he was expected to provide for a subdeacon!

(296) and (800) The Warden of the Leper Hospital

The Priory started the hospital of St. Mary Magdalene for lepers and other sick people in 1208. It was on the east side of South

Street on the town boundary, the town side of (today's) Half Moon Lane.

About 1208 Richard de Morins appointed Roger the Chaplain as Warden, with 'spiritual care and also custody of our hospital'. He was to be allowed '. . . that every day in the chapel of that place, to celebrate divine office . . . by permission of the mother church . . .' but 'on feast days which are held in the parish . . .' [when the townspeople will receive] 'summons to the mother church, and to make their gifts, no one of the parish shall be acceptable in the said chapel, whether for offering or giving, except that he send on such to his church'. The Charter states firmly that all tithes or gifts must be given 'whole and undiminished' to the mother church! This may account for the lack of gifts to this hospital, among the Priory Charters.

The Almonry and The Leper Hospital

These occur in several of the Charters but have long since disappeared. The hospital was on the northern side of the town boundary, now Half Moon Lane. The Almonry was probably on the western side of the market place and, unless it was moved in later years, to the north of the site which in 1259 would be taken over by the Friary. There were several gifts to the Almonry, recorded in the Charters; (595) and (599) are the gifts of Paul Piper and in (402) the 'daughters of Thirkell' gave land to 'the Hospital of St. John the Baptist near the court of the Canons'. The gift is described as being at the end of their court[yard] and '40 feet in length from the Hospital towards the west . . .' In (594) they gave another 168 feet from the end of their court. This second gift is to the Hospital of St. Peter but is probably an alternative name for the same building. It is impossible to fix a site from such vague details but in the 15th century the newly formed Fraternity of businessmen was dedicated to St. John the Baptist. They had an almshouse and other property in West Street. There are no references to the Almonry in later centuries but in the early 13th century there were a number of gifts including land to build a dovehouse. Hundreds of years later there was still a small field called Dovehouse Close.

Chapter 4

The Work of an Augustinian Priory

Not only the Benedictines but most other religious houses based their Rule and way of life on that which St. Benedict gave his followers in the 5th century. Although he ordered them to take a vow of poverty, chastity and obedience, he also encouraged them to make and support beautiful churches and to treat the stranger at their gate as though it was Christ himself who stood there. To build and maintain churches, to supply hospitality, to treat the sick and to distribute alms required a great deal of money. Long before the 13th century they had to accept that although they were individually without so much as a pair of shoes to call their own, communally they must somehow arrange for an adequate income. Some houses, such as the Cistercians at Woburn and (Old) Warden, deliberately chose isolated sites, where there were few travellers or parishioners, and originally they did most of the unskilled work themselves rather than employ lay brothers, who would add to the need for an unnecessarily large church building. In fact this didn't last, for their successful farming ventures soon required the help of lay brothers.

The Need For Money
The Augustinian Rule was in many ways similar to that of the Benedictines but each canon was an ordained priest and many of them had a second training such as teaching or music. They were expected to provide for a parish church at or near their own house and also to travel around their district taking

services. As at Dunstable many Augustinian houses were on main roads, and the care of all travellers, rich and poor, sick and disabled, was an important part of their work.

The seven services of the monastic day set the framework of their life. In addition they undertook many hours of private prayer on behalf of the sick and those who had recently died; for which they sometimes received a little money. The writing of music and new settings of the mass, the copying of music, mass books and sections of the Bible were also an important part of their work and this brought in a little money, but not enough.

The Income of the Priory

Travellers were expected to leave money to pay for their lodgings and to put coins in the poor box, but most of the money used by the canons to support their work came indirectly from gifts and bequests. These were needed to help pay the running costs of the hostel and the almonry and to maintain and beautify the church. They also received gifts in practical ways such as wax for candles, wheat for bread, or malt and barley to brew beer; but the main working income of Dunstable Priory and of most other religious houses was the income that they could collect as rents or incomes from the many gifts of land and houses that they received.[1]

However, these gifts of property brought many responsibilities, e.g. when King Henry I gave his new royal town of Dunstable to the Priory they also took on manorial responsibility, and had either to take over the secular duties of Lord of the Manor, or employ a steward to act for them.

Gifts poured in and they soon had secular and religious duties in many of the villages of south and mid Bedfordshire as well as in several other counties. Their income from the town of Dunstable depended on maintaining a prosperous market and trading centre, so they encouraged a great deal of development. Although like many other religious houses the Priory probably

---

1   B.H.R.S. Vol. X. The Charters of Dunstable Priory.

had members or stewards who studied and put into practice new methods of farming, their income from agricultural land was extremely unreliable, because it was so dependent on good weather. When harvests were bad, crops from every available strip of land were needed to support the canons and their dependants through the winter. This desperate need for income and especially food meant that they had to be scrupulous at recording all gifts and occasional exchanges of land. Despite their unworldly background the canons had to be ruthless in protecting their property.

For example, at their foundation King Henry I had given them part of the Manor of Houghton. Later King Henry II gave another part to one of his Norman barons, Hugh de Gurnay. When from time-to-time Hugh quarreled with King Henry II, or King John, the Prior was given the whole Manor of Houghton, but when Hugh was forgiven he got his land back again. As the years went by the Prior became increasingly reluctant to give it up and around 1220, after his representative had occupied the manor house, alongside the church, for several years, he refused to give it up. De Gurnay became so furious that he sent his men to destroy the house and had a new moated manor house built at Thorn[1]. The Prior was so jealous of his lost estate that he sought permission from the King to build his own moated manor house, at Calcutt, south of Chalgrave. (The Thorn house was pulled down long before living memory and the Calcutt house in 1975, but the remains of both moats can be seen on the Ordnance Survey Map.)

The Prior continually petitioned King John and in 1223 was given one-third of all the woodland, including Buckwood. (See 'The Treatise' below.) The published Charters and the 'Treatise of the Priory' are a very valuable source of information to both local and national historians. One reason why records were kept so carefully was that disputes could occur; occasionally the donor's son or grandson would dispute the gift.

---

1   B.H.R.S. Vol. IXX. The Treatise of Dunstable Priory.

The Charters and Other Documents

When the religious houses were closed in the 16th century, the numerous books, charters, documents and music were scattered and sometimes even destroyed. Although within fifty years their interest and importance was recognised by scholars who searched for them, and began to build up private collections, many were already lost. More about their adventures, before they finally reached public archives, will be included in a later book.

Three sets of manuscripts from Dunstable Priory were saved.

1. The Annals – an annual account of the main local and national events. The original in the British Museum and the published edition which is most readily available, printed in 1866, along with many other such documents, is in Latin.[1] However, there are some pages of translation available at the Bedfordshire County Record Office.

The regular annual entries start in 1202, the year that Richard de Morins became prior, and continue until 1297. By that time the Priory was going through a long troubled period, when priors changed quite frequently, and after that date there were only occasional entries, which ended, altogether in 1459.

The length and the amount of details given in each entry varies very much and it is sometimes frustrating to find which facts the writer has selected to include and which he has ignored.

There is a regular record of the deaths of kings and church officials and a fairly reliable record of the visits of royal parties and of senior church officials. On April 19, 1220, Bishop Robert, of Lismore '. . . dedicated the church of Studham and five altars in it and consecrated and extended [the] churchyard . . . On the preceding day at Dunstable he had dedicated the altar of the Holy Cross in honour of All Angels and a parish altar in honour of St. John the Baptist'. The entry goes on to record the dedication of Chalgrave and Pulloxhill churches and that the

---

1   The Annales Prioratus de Dunstaplia published in the Annales Monastic Series.

Bishop of Lincoln also visited the Priory, during the same month.

There are occasional references to the priory building, such as in 1222 when the presbytery roof collapsed in June and was repaired, only for the two towers, 'at the front of Dunstable church to collapse six months later, seriously damaging the prior's hall and the church'. The cause of this latter damage was a great gale which caused damage over several counties.

West front of the Priory Church of St. Peter showing the great Norman door and the 'new' Early English door beside it. O.R.

As far as the town of Dunstable is concerned there are several references to the struggle mentioned in Chapter 6 but the annals cannot be relied upon as a source of information because one is often disappointed by the absence of comments. Although the regular entries had ended before the great plague of 1349 (the Black Death), one would have thought that writing in a market town which relied heavily on travellers for its income, the distress and disruption would have justified quite a long entry, but all the writer chose to record was that the townsmen paid for a new bell to be made and called it Mary. This bell can still be seen at the back of the present church.

The writers were always interested in any unusual phenomenon that they heard of. During the winter of the great storm a comet was frequently seen in both England and France; sometimes '. . . it glowed red in a remarkable way'. There are other references to both storms and to stars and also to 'Fireycrosses' which were seen in the sky but they also recorded less creditable pieces of information. The long entry for 1221 includes the information that '. . . it was commonly said that at Melford in Essex a cow gave birth to a child in human form!'[1]

Nevertheless despite these criticisms the Annals of Dunstable Priory are an amazing collection of local and national events, covering most of the 13th century.

2. The Charters. – published as B.H.R.S. X, are records concerning the gifts that the Priory received, a few purchases and exchanges and some interesting passages such as the terms under which they appointed a gaoler – (see below). The originals are now in the British Museum as part of the collection made by Robert Harley, 1st Earl of Oxford. The Duncombe family of Battlesden owned them in the early 17th century and later in that century a London vintner bought them and paid to have them bound. By the early 18th century the Rev. J. Clithero, Vicar of Houghton Regis, held them. He also had a living at Holkham in Norfolk and it appears that he retired to that county and took them with him. By 1716 they were safely in the Harlean collection.[2] B.H.R.S. Vol.X is mainly in Latin but there are enough notes in English to make it extremely interesting and useful. (See below.)

3. The Treatise – published in English as B.H.R.S. IXX, is a collection of notes and interesting pieces of information put together about 1280–1290, some of which are included below. There are several entries concerning the large wood, known as Buckwood, which bounded the Watling Street at Markyate.

---

1   I am grateful to Mrs Liz North for access to her translations of this part of the Annals.

2   Davies, G.R., Medieval Cartularies of Great Britain.

(The remaining portion of the wood is now known as Beechwood.) King Henry I gave the farmers of Houghton Regis that wood to make up for the land that they lost when he founded his new town. (The short path near the Saracen's Head, in Dunstable, once called Woodway and now Wood Street, is a remaining part of the right of way from Houghton to Buckwood.) These rights were often in dispute and continued to be so after the Dissoluton. During the winter 1619-20, the Ferrars family who were the new owners of Markyate Cell were in dispute with a group of local men who claimed rights in the wood. The Treatise was produced as evidence; and then became part of the documentary records of the Beechwood estate, until they were bought by the British Records Association in 1935 and from them passed to the Bedford County Record Office. Unfortunately the surviving parchments are only a small part of the original documents.[1]

Other Work Undertaken by the Canons

Farming. It is most unlikely that the canons ever had to work on their agricultural land. Most of it would have been let out to tenants and even if they used their land at Houghton Regis as a home farm they would have employed a steward or farm bailiff. However they would have studied the latest farming methods and also marketing; one or more canons would have made sure that their land was being well farmed and used for whatever type of farming was most profitable.

Growing Herbs. Although we have no written records to tell us about the herb gardens, or about the work of Dunstable's equivalent of Shrewsbury's fictitious Brother Cadfael, we can assume that there was always one experienced gardener.

Medical Work. In the excellent books of historical fiction, written by Ellis Peters, Brother Cadfael grows the herbs, makes the various medicines and delivers them to the brother who cares for the sick monks and to the Master of the Leper Hospital, who looks after sick travellers. In addition, he himself

---

1   Davies, G.R. op. cit.

carries them into the town of Shrewsbury and acts as doctor to the townspeople.

These stories are set in the 12th century. In Dunstable these duties may have been divided, especially by the mid 14th century, when understanding of both ill health and of its treatment was improving. As there were sometimes young canons studying at Oxford University they may have met medical students and possibly have visited the nursery garden, which by the 13th century was selling plants and seeds. Some of the canons therefore were probably familiar with the latest methods of treatment.

Dr John of Gaddesden. When a monastery was founded in the middle of Ashridge Forest, in 1283, one of the witnesses was John of Gaddesden. He may well have lived on the site of the present 'John of Gaddesden's House', opposite the gates of Ashridge House. It was probably his son, another John, who was born around 1280, who studied at Merton College Oxford and graduated as Doctor of Medicine in 1309[1].

He was one of the leading doctors of his day and his knowledge of medicine was held in high esteem. He was called upon to treat patients for Kings Edward I and II and travelled with royal parties in both England and France. He is best known today because he wrote England's first medical text book. As Chaucer recorded in the Canterbury Tales, the doctor could make a great deal of money out of medicine. However, it is also recorded that he would treat poor people free-of-charge.

John of Gaddesden and Dunstable. It is most unlikely that John received his early teaching at The Priory School because his family had connections with St. Albans Abbey but, travelling to and fro to Oxford, when escorting royal parties, or when he was visiting Little Gaddesden or Berkhamsted, he may well have stayed at the Priory.

His 'Modern' Medicine. His text book was called 'Rosa Medicinae' because the rose had five sepals and the book had five parts.

---

1   Howard Senar. Little Gaddesden and Ashridge.

Some of his teaching, which may seem to us to have been of little value, would have been accepted by the canons. For an aching tooth – 'When the Sunday Gospel is read, let the man sign his tooth and his head with the sign of the cross and say a Paternoster and an Ave for the souls of the father and mother of St. Philip without stopping. It will keep the teeth from pain in the future and cure them in the present'. However, his suggestion that the dried and powdered body of a dead cuckoo would cure epilepsy or that paralysis would be cured if the affected limb was bathed in water in which a whole fox had been boiled, until the flesh separated from the bones, may have tested their credulity, even if the water did contain rue and peonies!

Health Care at The Priory Hostel. Having cast doubts on some of Gaddesden's medicine, much of his advice was sensible and would have been of great use to the canons at the Priory. He understood that tuberculosis led to severe damage of the lungs and could not be cured. He treated such patients in the early stages by advising them to avoid the germs of coughs and colds, and to prevent coughing by using soothing drinks and ointments. To build up their strength he recommended tempting the appetite and encouraging sleep.

For treating the many travellers who arrived at the hostel or almonry having had a fall from a horse or having been attacked along the road, Gaddesden would have recommended:

(i) Remove any weapon or foreign body.
(ii) Stop the bleeding.
(iii) Carefully put tissues back together.
(iv) Cut away any infected tissues.
(v) Select a suitable dressing.
(vi) If necessary, bleed and give a calming draught.
(vii) If severe swelling follows bathe and treat to reduce the swelling.
(viii) Encourage the patient to rest.

It had always been thought necessary to keep the wounds connected with broken bones open but he encouraged the careful positioning of the broken bone, then of the torn flesh, before stitching it in place and treating as above.

However, it was his advice for all travellers which the canons would have found particularly useful. Travellers should:

(i) Before leaving home give attention to health and don't travel unless in good health.

(ii) When travelling in hot weather resist the heat and avoid drinking water, by eating sugared rose petals, violets or chicory, chewing tamarinde, barbery or sorrel, sipping an infusion of sandle wood in water, or flavoured vinegar.

(iii) If the air is hot and smelly, inhale camphor, musk, roses or herbs. If it is very offensive, hold your nose while sipping aromatic wines.

(iv) If very cold on arrival, do not rush to the fire but rub limbs and warm up gradually.

(v) Always bathe feet in hot water, in which fennel or camomile have been boiled and make quite sure they are dry, before going to bed.

(vi) Drink wine made from the roots of wormwood, to relive fatigue.

(vii) Before leaving the next morning, have a good breakfast of roast meat and garlic, with a good wine.

(viii) Before setting out the next morning wash the feet in hot salt water, dry them and then rub in fat from a goat, or ram. If this fat is not available, use oil of linseed or even candle wax.

(ix) If travelling in winter wear a garment made of two layers of fabric with an inner layer of cotton wadding, cover this with a shirt lined with fox, lamb or rabbit skin. On the head wear a cap lined with fur and then a hood which comes right over the top and down on to the shoulders. Also try and keep the feet warm and dry.

(x) In summer keep the head covered to avoid sunstroke.

Chapter 5

The Thirteenth Century Town

The Priory Charters (B.H.R.S. X)

From these we can learn a lot about Dunstable in the early 13th century. The Priory was a royal foundation and, as the town prospered, the burgesses and others showered it with gifts. The humble gave a little, a rent of a shilling or up to half an acre of land, the great gave a lot. Robert of Huntingdon who held an official position at Belvoir Castle (to whom the village of Studham belonged) granted 'his dearest lords and brothers the canons' £5.16s. from the rent in Dunstable and part of his goods. In return for this the canons were to bring his body back to Dunstable and bury it honourably.

Also recorded are various notes of business and domestic affairs concerning the Priory:

596. 'John son of William the blacksmith, holds land in the market place between the shop of Henry son of Theodore and the smithy of William son of Reginald'. This occurred in the first quarter of the 13th century and suggests that what became known as 'Middle Rents' – later Middle Row, had begun to be built.

292. 'Richard Prior of Dunstable, grants to Alan the goldsmith, a plot on which to build 18ft x 14ft at a rent of three shillings per year, next to the workshop of Gilbert'.

295. 'Flemengus the Jew of London . . . he and his son and his servants have permission to come and to stay in Dunstable with all the liberties of the vill. For this they will pay yearly, 2 silver spoons each 12d. weight'. Jews were allowed by their religion to

lend money and in some ways acted as banks. This was not popular and they were open to exploitation. During the reign of Edward I they were obliged to leave England. All the goldsmiths and named Jews had left Dunstable by the tax list of 1297.

301. At some date between 1225–50 the Priory made an agreement to sell fleeces for 6d. (2½p!) each for the next six years. This was very risky. By fixing the price for six years they may have got an extra farthing (¼ penny) per fleece, at the time but if prices went up they would not benefit. Some religious houses who had got into financial difficulties fell into an even worse trap. They accepted an 'advance' from the dealer on their next year's wool. At the best they were short of income but if they lost sheep in the snow, or there was disease in the flock, the little wool they did have for sale, the following year, might not even cancel out the debt.

Wool was an important part of the Priory's income. Not only did they have grazing on the Downs around Dunstable but a grateful traveller had given their hostel a valuable sheep farm in Bradbourne, Derbyshire.

507. 'May those present and future know that we Richard the Prior and Monastery of Dunstable, grant and desire that William son of Ralph and his heirs should be our free man . . .' For this freedom from villeinage (an unfree man being forced to work for his landlord instead of paying rent) he paid 3d. In future, he and his heirs would pay a money rent and enjoy other privileges*. This is an interesting example of a man buying his freedom.

The Town Around the Crossroads

Most of the charters are straightforward gifts of rents from land, or a messuage (which is a house with dependent buildings, a yard, or maybe even one or two workers' cottages), or a tenement, which is purely residential. Having studied these charters and sorted owners from tenants to avoid duplication, I have been able to draw some conclusions about

---

*   I am grateful to Mrs Joan Schneider for translating this charter.

the town in the early thirteenth century but they must not be regarded as an entirely accurate account.

The roads were called North, South, East and West Street. The houses lined the roads, many having courtyards with outhouses, servants' cottages, warehouses, craft workshops, and maybe enclosed land or paddocks behind them. The only lanes mentioned are (795) from the mill in West Street to the north, and (282) from the house of Angerus (South Street?) to the Priory. This may be the path still featured on the first Ordinance Survey Map, running approximately from the High Street end of the present Britain Street.

Behind these properties filling in the land to the boundary on each corner of the town was the inland, small parcels of land privately owned by many different people. Outside the boundary, to where the town land met the land of the next village, were the outlands or open fields, divided into strips and shared by the Priory and some of the burgesses.

Dunstable was not a walled town and no ditch has ever been found, so the boundaries are hard to identify. According to an old charter, quoted in the Treatise of the Priory, Henry I made the town four square with a ploughland (a vague term meaning perhaps about 120 acres) on each corner. Britain Street was a likely town boundary; Englands Lane, often a corruption of 'Inlands', would have continued and come out between today's Priory Road and Station Road. There is one messuage mentioned east of the town graveyard. This must have continued at least part-way across what is now Priory Road as recent excavations by the Manshead Archaeological Society, uncovered part of the graveyard in a local garden. Property belonging to the Priory filled most of this quarter; there are charters where the canons let out land behind the houses. The leper hospital was on the town boundary now called Half Moon Lane* which probably eventually came out on East Street, by the Long Hedge, now Station Road, marked by Worthington Smith.

---

*   A later name associated with the Half Moon Inn, now Bernard Hughes Furniture Designer and Manufacturer.

Opposite, most of the quarter was taken up by the king's land and the paddocks of the business houses lining East Street and the crossroads end of North Street. There was a little privately owned inland; Ralph Bunyan gave the Priory an acre of his inlands near the king's court (yard). Further along North Street the outlands may have been a shared rectangle of ploughland called Long Furlong, but the fields of Houghton came nearly up to the town. Union Street was probably the boundary with the land of Houghton and the charters suggest that 'Dunstable' smallholdings continued to the border where they met 'Houghton' smallholdings.

On the west side of North Street was the West Field. Again, the boundary is unknown, but medieval documents suggest a path or boundary from Union Street round to Leighton Gap, which was the headland round the West Field and became the road to Totternhoe and Leighton.

The Young family owned most of West Street; the windmill, land and also at least two messuages. Ralph Young was a wool exporter, his grandfather, Alexander, gave the Priory four shops and ten houses and his great uncle, John, had a farm. We do not know exactly where the Young family had their farmhouse but it is tempting to suggest that it was on the site of the building now standing on the corner of West Street and Matthew Street and also the western end of Knowles Benning. Up until Matthew Gutteridge laid out Matthew Street, on what had been the entrance to his farm yard, and sold off his farmyard, rickyard (haystacks) and Home Close (small field) for building (Matthew/Victoria Street) in 1865, that site had been a working farm for many hundreds of years.

The other side of West Street was the Kensworth Field, perhaps stretching from Icknield Street/Bull Pond Lane up to 'Catchacre'. This is one of several names given to a piece of disputed land, in this case between Dunstable Priory land and that of St. Paul's, at Kensworth. Over the years there were several paths across this field. Part of Canesworde Road was once a path leading to Kensworth, the spelling of Kensworth in 1086 being 'Canesworde'. The dates of these different paths, marked on Worthington Smith's map, are unknown. On the Tithe Map of 1836 a pond is marked in Bull Pond Piece. This was on the west wide of the lane, opposite what was once the Friary*. The Tithe Map also marks long strips of land from South Street up to Bull Pond Lane and others on the western side. These may have been the traditional inlands. Canesworde Road may have been the headland around the Kensworth Field.

The general impression drawn from the Charters is that West Street had shops and business houses near the crossroads and then smaller houses. Above (today's) Icknield Street was the Kensworth Field and above Princes Street lay enclosed paddocks and small fields up to the mill, with West Field laying behind and beyond. The mill and four houses are mentioned and four shops and ten houses suggested.

The west side of South Street started with the market. The Middle Row that we know, with stone-built shops, was not there and houses are not mentioned, but some of the craft workshops may have been lathe and plaster with living accommodation above. Nine shops are mentioned, including two goldsmiths, a blacksmith and a workshop. There were of course many more, some being simply portable barrows. After the market came the larger and more important messuages; then there were small houses and enclosed paddocks, up to the boundary.

On the east side, the Priory had twelve houses, mainly small with rents of 3d. (1¼p) to 2/- (10p) each; possibly from the gates of the great courtyard, south towards Britain Street. The Porter's Lodge was probably south of the gates, with the hospitium or hostel (columns of which can be seen in Priory House) lying north towards the crossroads. There may have been some business houses between Church Walk and the crossroads. Eighteen houses are mentioned, three with land behind and one with a marlpit; thirteen more are suggested, five messuages are mentioned, two members of the Young family, a carter and a baker.

---

* This is not the Friar's Pond, which was in the middle of South Street, near the Saracen's Head.

As the Priory and the king's houses took up most of East Street (Church Street) there are few references to this road in the Charters. After King John gave Kingsbury to the Priory in 1210, the Prior leased to Walter, son of Aldewi, an establishment in the courtyard big enough to be described as a messuage. Walter, son of the miller, had a messuage between the Priory and the boundary. Three messuages are mentioned, and two houses, four others are suggested.

There must have been business houses around the crossroads and on either side of North Street, but they are not mentioned except for references to Richard Weston, the merchant, and to John the Cooper and Picot the Carter, whose property may have been in North Street. Only two messuages are named and three houses but more than thirty houses are suggested, many of them occupied by tradesmen and craftsmen. The general impression is that a handful of wealthy traders owned houses and businesses along the street and that just as in the nineteenth century each one had a very large courtyard, lined with cottages and small businesses.

Simon, son of John, who *may* have been son of John of Houghton, Archdeacon of Bedford, owned several properties in North Street. He gave many gifts to the Priory but his gifts of tenements are mixed with gifts of land and the gifts of his under-tenants giving their legal share of the same houses, which makes it impossible to do an accurate count. Several other people also gave land and tenement rents.

The paddocks and small holdings were near the boundary, with Long Furlong behind them on the east and West Field behind on the west. There are eight assorted houses mentioned in North Street and another thirty-five suggested.

Altogether there is evidence of one hundred and two houses and thirteen shops, total one hundred and fifteen, not including burgess property not connected with the Priory and the numerous cottages around the courtyards. The tax of 1297, which also disregarded the poor people who lived in these cottages, listed one hundred and twenty-one households and the rent list of 1542, which again may ignore many of the courtyard cottages, lists approximately two hundred households. The tax list of 1671, which listed every house, totalled two hundred and twelve[1]. These 13th century figures can only be used as a general impression and can in no way be used to produce an accurate assessment of population. They were compiled by plotting property mentioned as gifts and tenancies plus neighbouring properties, used as identification.

The Tax Report of 1297 (Published as B.H.R.S. XXXIX)

In 1085-6 the 'Domesday' tax was concerned with collecting money from the large landowners; land and property values, income from markets, courts, etc. By the late thirteenth century there were far more towns, like Dunstable, where the economy was based on trade, not agriculture. An inventory was made of people's livestock and their stock of raw materials; from these assessments we can draw a comparative picture between different towns and villages. Bedford was the county administrative centre, Leighton and Luton small market towns and Dunstable a flourishing business centre. The tax was not on houses but on goods and anyone who did not have livestock, stocks of raw materials, or goods for sale was not included. One hundred and twenty one households were taxed which covered all the business, trade and artisan houses, but not the workers' cottages around the courtyards. Some of the burgess families who made gifts to the Priory are still there sixty or seventy years later; others are not listed but if daughters had inherited these businesses they may be there but under their husband's name. John Durrant recently deceased was the most prosperous resident; he was a wool exporter and owned one hundred sheep, a bull, six cows and a store of wood. This was at a time when it was necessary to have a licence to export wool. Of the few names entered as licensed export merchants, in the state papers, John and five others came from Dunstable[2].

---

1   B.H.R.S. Vol. XVI. Mrs Marshall estimates a lower figure, based on the style of recording but this does not seem likely.
2   J. Godber. The History of Bedfordshire, p.62.

Apart from wool the main industries were corn and hides. In his introduction to B.H.R.S. XXXIX, A. T. Gaydon suggests that there may have been twenty households in some way dealing in cereals. There were ten tanners, eight dealers in skins, a curer of skins, a man dealing in woollen felt, four blacksmiths, and a carter, with a cart and four 'affers', (beasts of burden). A carpenter and a tiler had stores of timber and Adam le Cous had 4–5,000 tiles and some lime. When in 1309 the monastery at Winchester wanted to build a new barn, on their estates at Ivinghoe, they bought 900 lathes in Dunstable for 9s.0d. (45p). They also bought 52,800 tiles, together with lime for £6.8s.5½d. Tiles were priced from 2s.4d. (11½p) to 2s.8d. (13½p) per 1,000[1].

There was a brewer, five butchers, five fishmongers, poulterer, two bakers, a fruiterer and a spicer. Although there would have been a workshop at the Priory making both beeswax and mutton fat candles, there was sufficient demand to support a specialist candle maker in the town.

Surprisingly few sheep were listed; were it not that the tax rolls for many of the villages are missing, we would probably find some of the Dunstablians taxed for their sheep in Caddington, Kensworth, Chalgrave and Houghton.

These few paragraphs show what a prosperous commercial centre the new town of Dunstable had become by 1300, with the residents not only working in the town but also travelling and trading all over this country and overseas.

New Arrivals

Some religious orders, e.g. the Cistercians, at Woburn, deliberately chose isolated sites on which to build, but a new order had arrived in England who were looking for land in prosperous market towns – the Dominicans. The Augustinian Canons had been in the town since soon after its foundation and had actively sponsored its development. The people of Dunstable attended their services, gave tithes and other

---

1   Z.Tetow. Manorial Documents. p.203.

offerings and, as at that time England was a Roman Catholic country, paid for confessions and for personal and family prayers and services, particularly on the day of a funeral and at set intervals afterwards. The canons would bitterly resent any new intruders, with whom they must share these financial privileges.

Saint Domininc

St. Dominic was himself an Augustinian Canon from Castille, in Spain, when he travelled through some of the poorest parts of France. Like the Dunstable canons he personally was without any money or property but as a member of an Augustinian house, he wore well made clothes and instead of walking rode on a horse. When night fell he would leave the road and sleep in a monastery or other respectable place.

Away from his House and passing through some of the poorest villages he had ever seen, he began to realise that the social gap between these people and even the poorest monk or canon was far too great for them ever to be able to communicate, such that in order to win their condfience and teach them about the love of God he must change his entire life.

The Dominican Friars

Soon afterwards he founded what became known as the Order of Dominican Friars. They made no attempt either to build up large, income-creating estates or, in small towns like Dunstable, to run hostels, hospitals or schools. They relied on the message of Christ and set out without money or food, providing for themselves and for others with the alms that they were given. Often they were licensed to collect money at inns, crossroads or beside major roads.

They Came to Dunstable. The Order expanded very rapidly and in 1221, Dominic and his advisors decided to send some of their followers to England. They were in London by August and shortly afterwards opened their first English house at Oxford. By 1259 the town of Dunstable had become so prosperous that Henry III and his Queen, Eleanor of Provence, persuaded the Augustinians, much against their will, to let the friars settle there. Both church and gatehouse faced on to South Street, right opposite the Priory gateway, so they were separated only by the road and what became known as the 'Friar's Pond'[1].

Their entire estate consisted of three cottages along their South Street boundary, their own buildings, courtyard and gardens, plus a large orchard, to the west, in the direction of the present Bennetts Recreation Ground and four acres in the adjoining Kensworth Field[2]. In 1286 a fourth cottage near their boundary came up for sale and although the friars would have liked to have bought it, the Prior arranged for his porter to do so, thus preventing them.

Matthew Paris, the chronicler at St. Albans Abbey, made scathing remarks about their lavish buildings. A. R. Martin, writing in the Manshead Magazine of 1966, noted that 'excessive extravagence' was most unlikely and excavations by the Society in 1966 and 1967 seemed to support this view[3]. However, later excavations by a Bedfordshire County Council Archaeological team in 1990 uncovered a surprisingly large church.

The arrival must have caused a great deal of worry, not to mention jealousy, across at the Priory. King Henry wrote to the Prior on 9th April, 1259 and again on 27th October, asking that the canons should be charitable and friendly towards the new arrivals – but it was not easy. Martin set out the various recorded quarrels between the two rival houses and noted many of the gifts they received. During the first half of the 13th century the three King Edwards, direct descendents of the founder of the Friary, Henry III, all sent generous gifts, as did many other rich people. What was more worrying to the Augustinians was the way local people diverted their alms and

---

1   This was in the middle of the road, near the Saracen's Head, a stretch of road still liable to flooding. I am grateful to Whitbread & Co. plc for permission to study the deeds of the Saracen's Head.
2   B.H.R.S. Vol. 64.
3   M.A.S. Magazines. Vols. 16 and 17.

bequests and rewarded the friars for hearing their confessions and holding special services to commemorate the lives of their loved ones.

Until the friars came to Dunstable most people from the town and surrounding villages made their gifts to God via the Priory; now these gifts were either divided or went entirely to the friars. We can trace these gifts from surviving wills[1]. However whereas most donors to the Priory are comparatively local, those to the Friary are also found coming from families in the surrounding counties.

One of the earliest gifts to the Friary, which the canons could have expected to receive, was that from Thomas le Blunde. Earlier in the century his family had given property to the Priory, but in 1262 he let the friars have land at a nominal rent of one penny per year. The arrangement was registered when the king's judges came to Dunstable Priory, on 14th May. In return, Thomas and his wife Justine, were to receive 'all benefactions and prayers made henceforth in his [Prior of the Friary] church, of St. Mary'. To add to the bitterness of the Prior, the spokesman who represented the Friary, Richard Young was probably grandson of Alexander, who had been a major benefactor earlier in the century [2].

Dunstable in the 13th Century – A Traveller's View

By 1300 travellers coming into the town from the south would have been impressed first by the Leper Hospital of St. Mary, with its own chapel, standing on the right, then the well-cultivated paddocks and small fields on either side of the road and as they got nearer the town, large houses and warehouses on the left and smaller but well maintained houses belonging to the Priory on the right. Visible from a great distance, standing in the middle of the crossroads was the Eleanor Cross, towering above the surrounding houses with its brilliant reds, blues, gold leaf and gilding, still clean, shiny and bright. As travellers approached the crossroads the Friary

1   See B.H.R.S. Vols. XXXVII and XLV.
2   B.H.R.S. Vol. VI, part II, 624.

Church was on the left and the Priory gatehouse and hostel on the right, with the even bigger Priory Church and buildings visible through the open gate.

The market still consisted of moveable stalls but it is possible that the market hall was in the process of being built. The foundations and some of the timbers of this building may be incorporated in number 26 High Street South. 'Middle Rents', the permanent craft workrooms and shops gradually developed into Middle Row and were built during the following fifty to a hundred years.

Once past the Eleanor Cross the visitor could look to the left into West Street and see prosperous shops and houses on either side of a pond and a wide open space, where the sheep market was held. To the right, he could see the Priory Church, Kingsbury and numerous small, neat cottages and shops. Ahead a long straight road lined on either side with big residential houses stretched into the distance. If could have looked into the yards behind, he would have seen warehouses, malting sheds, barns, stables, cart sheds and numerous cottages.

Dunstable had come a long way since Prior Richard de Morins had been elected in 1202.

Chapter 6

Dunstable Suffers During
The Fight for Magna Carta – 1215

Civil wars are particularly distressing, not just because loyalty to a cause, or enforced participation, divides both families and communities but also because, as the two armies cross and recross the different counties, forage and livestock are 'compulsory purchased', with promissory notes for payment instead of cash. Houses and barns are robbed and young men are both legally and illegally conscripted or even taken by force. These unsettled conditions encourage civil unrest and gradually law and order breaks down. These events started before the struggle between the Priory and the burgesses but continued well into that period and may have aggravated the situation.

Dunstable, placed as it is on the crossing of two main routes, north/south and east/west, suffered particularly badly. During the English Civil Wars of the 12th and 13th centuries, many mercenaries were brought into England from the continent. These 'foreign' soldiers were even less likely to treat the countryside with respect particularly if, as often happened, wages and supplies were late arriving. A mercenary castle at Luton added to the problems of the burgesses of Dunstable[1].

The 1220s must have been a particularly difficult decade in which to live in Dunstable – the town on the crossroads!

---

1   Not the castle which gave Castle Street its name but on the riverside
     near St. Mary's Church. See Dyer, Stygall and Dony, The Story of Luton.

King John and Magna Carta

In the 13th century kings had great power. Barons and other landowners had to pay rent to the king and when they died their heir had to pay a 'relief' (inheritance fee)*. If there was no direct heir the king might claim the inheritance; or if the heir was a minor the king might take all the profits from his estates; or 'sell' the guardianship of a minor, or the remarriage of a widow, so that someone else could benefit by their estates. These very wide powers were selfishly used by King John to rob many of his subjects. This was just one of many ways that he damaged their property and incomes. Also in the first fourteen years of his reign, he had repeatedly involved England in fighting overseas, despite which he had lost most of the land which England held in France.

As kings could also get rents and reliefs from churches and religious houses and John had made himself unpopular with them, he interfered with privileges which had traditionally belonged to the Pope and, as England was a Roman Catholic Country, the Pope was able to put an interdict over England and for six years the churches stood silent and unused – there were no bells and no services.

It was not long before King John had alienated the army, the clergy, the religious houses and all levels of secular society, so for his own safety he brought foreign mercenaries into England, which added to his unpopularity. Gradually the country was slipping towards Civil War. Later the Pope encouraged the King of France to invade England and to try and take the throne. John was obliged to go through a humiliating ceremony whereby he handed the crown of England to the Pope.

To try and avoid war, groups of church and secular leaders gathered on August 4th 1213, at St. Albans Abbey, where they discussed what could be done. Eventually it was decided to get King John to sign a list of 'Articles' based on the ancient laws of the realm, ascribed traditionally to Edward the Confessor and included in the Coronation Charter of Henry I.

---

*　　Tenants of the landowners had to pay them a similar inheritance fee, see the Young family above.

Arbitration proved useless and eventually the barons raised an army to enforce their wishes. In June 1215 they were camped at Staines and the King and his mercenaries at Windsor; they met in a field by the River Thames, called 'Runnymede', and after yet more discussion King John signed a list of sixty-three articles which soon became known as 'Magna Carta' or the great charter. It is still kept safely, with its great seal, in the British Library, together with several of the revisions which followed. Two of the many clauses which are still in use today read:

39) 'No freeman shall be seized or imprisoned or stripped of his rights or possessions . . . except by the lawful judgement of his equals or by the law of the land.'

40) 'To no one will we sell, to no one deny or delay right or justice'.

These articles which have benefitted Britain and much of the English speaking world were discussed, partly laid out, and fought for in our area. Local landowners and their men took part in the discussions, arbitration and finally the fighting.

Falkes de Breauté

One of the most notorious of King John's mercenaries was Falkes (or Faux) de Breauté, from Poitou, who is recorded during 1211 as leading a successful campaign in Wales. He remained a loyal supporter of King John and was one of the council appointed to advise the nine year old King Henry III.

In 1215 he laid siege to Bedford Castle, on behalf of King John, and when it surrendered became 'keeper'; in 1217 he broke the siege at Lincoln Castle, captured William de Beauchamp and as his reward was appointed Sheriff of Bedfordshire and Buckinghamshire in William's place. Eventually he was sheriff of seven counties and in charge of many castles. As a financial reward for his services, King John 'gave' him Margaret, widow of Baldwin de Rives, to be his wife. She owned land in south London where Falkes had a large house or hall built called Faux's or Vaux's Hall*. The name Vauxhall was brought back to Bedfordshire in 1905, by the Vauxhall Ironworks, later Vauxhall Motors Ltd.

By 1218 England was at peace and de Breauté's skills were no longer needed; he became restless and troublesome. In 1216 he had become Lord of the Manor of Luton and sometime after 1218 when they were no longer needed to defend the king, he and his soldiers terrorised the neighbourhood from a castle they had built somewhere between St. Mary's Church and the River Lea. The climax of his career occurred in 1224 when his soldiers kidnapped the king's judge, who was sitting at the Prior's court at Dunstable, (see below), and put him in the dungeons in Bedford Castle. King Henry laid siege to the castle while his officers escorted Falkes back from his hiding place at Chester. Because of his long years of loyalty and service his life was spared but he was exiled. He joined a crusade but died in 1226, at St. Ciriac in Southern France.

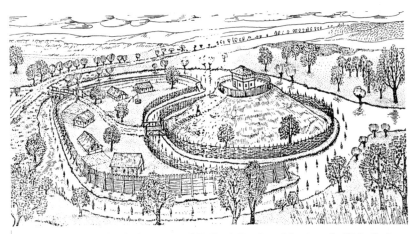

*An example of a simple 'Motte and Bailey' Castle, of the type built in Luton.
L.P.E.*

---

*   Falkes gave his name to part of London. E.Ekwall, 'The Concise Oxford Dictionary of England Place Names' mentions a spelling of what became Vauxhall, as 'Faukes-hal', in 1297. I am grateful to Dr David Shaw for pointing this out to me and also that several words in standard English have this voiced initial 'V' for the historic voiceless 'F' as in fox and vixen.

Local Military Leaders

As always with civil war, families were divided. William Marshall snr. had been closely connected with King Henry II, (and held the title of Earl Marshall of England) and, although sympathetic to the barons, having done his utmost to prevent war, supported Henry's son, King John.

William Marshall Jnr. had recently married the fourteen year old heiress to the manor of Luton. He supported the barons and played an active part from the beginning. Having joined them at Stamford, in February 1215, he marched with them to Bedford and then on to London where he left them to go to the coast to greet King Louis of France, who had arrived to claim the throne. He then joined the others at Staines and signed Magna Carta on behalf of the barons, while his father signed on behalf of the King. John immediately broke his promises so William Jnr. and some of the other barons continued to fight against him. As a result, when William's young wife died in 1216, King John appears to have taken Luton away from him and given it to Falkes de Breauté. William Jnr. retired to the family estates in Wales but came back after the death of King John to support the young King Henry III.

He remained loyal to Henry and was rewarded by the promise of marriage to Henry's baby sister Eleanor. William Marshall snr. died in May 1219 and William inherited the title. He married Eleanor in April 1224 when she was 9 years old! She was only sixteen when he died in 1231. At the time of their marriage Toddington was among the lands settled on him and he regained the manor of Luton in 1225. Eleanor became the Lady of the Manor until she married Simon de Montfort in January 1238, when it became part of her dowry.

Thomas Count of Perche and others at Toddington. Soon after 1066 Toddington was owned by a Norman family called de Hesding; it passed by marriage to Geoffrey Count of Perche, who died in 1203 leaving Toddington to his widow. The family lived in Normandy and when King John lost land in Normandy in 1204/5, the count's widow was obliged to surrender all their lands in England. King John gave the manor of Toddington to a foreign supporter Peter des Roches, Bishop of Winchester. Thomas Count of Perche, the deposed heir of Toddington, came to England with a small army, joined Prince Louis and was probably pleased to get his own back on the English king. He was eventually killed at the Battle of Lincoln.

Before 1200 another family called Pever had inherited land at Toddington. We do not know where their loyalty lay in 1215, but by 1249 when a Paul Pever was one of the senior civil servants, he supported Henry III against the barons in a later struggle. By that date he had become Lord of the Manor of Toddington.

William de Cantilupe, of Eaton [Bray] married, as his second wife, Millicent, daughter of Hugh de Gurney of Houghton Regis. When hostilities broke out, he was in a very difficult position because although his sympathies appear to have been with the barons he was seneschall, or steward, of King John's household. He was also Sheriff of Worcester, Leicester, Warwick and Hereford and was dependent on John for his generous income. He did not join the other barons at Bedford in 1215 but waited until they had successfully entered London and then went with them to Staines (Runnymede). When King John died he transferred his loyalty to the young King Henry and helped him relieve Lincoln Castle. In 1218 he was an itinerant justice in Bedfordshire but as custodian of Kenilworth Castle made that his main residence. Nevertheless, in 1221, probably in response to the continual raids of Falkes de Breauté's mercenaries at Luton, (see below) he pulled down the old manor house at Eaton and had a defended manor house or 'castle' built[1]. There was a defensive wall, a moat with two drawbridges and in the outer bailey was permanent stabling for sixty horses. Many medieval manor houses were built with a moat but for some reason de Cantilupe's defences were strong enough to give the contemporary name of 'castle'. By 1221 the soldiers of Faulkes de Breauté at Luton Castle were terrorising the neighbourhood and the annalist at Dunstable Priory

---

1   V.C.H. Beds. Vol. III, p.370.

recorded that the Priory and the neighbourhood were in danger from both castles!

His loyalty to the crown wavered again in 1224, when for a short time he supported the Earl of Chester's disagreement with the King but he soon returned to Henry at Northampton, was rewarded for his help at the seige at Bedford and was one of the signatories when Magna Carta was re-issued in 1236. He died at Reading in 1239 and was buried at Studely.

There is no record of fighting at Eaton and the 'castle' became neglected. A new manor house was built in the 16th century by the 'Bray' family who added their name to that of the village. The moat still survives on private land at Park Farm.

William de Beauchamp, Sheriff of Bedford. In 1215 William de Beauchamp, who was in charge of Bedford Castle, supported the barons and fought with them before and after the signing of Magna Carta. He was the organiser and senior officer for this part of England. Falkes de Breauté captured Bedford Castle in 1215 and held it for nine years, although William 'made his peace' with Henry III by the end of 1217. After the siege was broken in 1224 the site of the castle was returned to William but not until the trenches had been filled in and the castle walls removed. His new house was to have no military features. In later years he held several official appointments for King Henry but died in 1260 before the barons again rose against their King. His only surviving son, John was killed supporting Simon de Montfort at the Battle of Evesham in 1265.

Soldiers Pass Through Dunstable

During the many months of meetings and approaches to King John, who used every form of delaying tactics to avoid signing, large groups of armed soldiers marched through Dunstable. The charter was eventually signed, 'on or about June 15th 1215' and for a few months life returned to an uneasy peace but when a letter from the Pope encouraged King John to declare the charter illegal, fighting began all over again. This took the form of marching armies and castle sieges. As both Bedford and

Northampton Castles were attacked, soldiers continually passed through Dunstable. No doubt the burgesses and their workpeople suffered some damage but the presence of the Priory protected them from the worst outrages.

The Annals record, in 1215, some of the successes that Prince Louis, son of the King of France had had, since he arrived in England, which locally included the taking of Hertford and Berkhamsted Castles. The writer notes that Louis's army had caused 'great losses' in Dunstable and had received 200 marks (about £32). This was taken as a sort of protection money, because the Priory had given hospitality to King John and his army. He also suggests that about this time William Marshall Jnr. and some of the other barons became disillusioned with Louis and from then on he was, to a certain extent, acting independently.

King John died on October 19th 1215 and as the much respected William Marshall Snr. was one of the young King's (Henry III) advisers 'and because this King was young and guiltless and had harmed no one, many who had been at odds with [his] father began to support him'.

Nevertheless, within the entry for 1215, the writer records that, 'the Earl of Perche and the Marshal of France and 1,000 soldiers who Louis had given them, passed through Dunstable without doing much damage but then devastated everything, sparing neither windows nor churches'.

The Earl of Perche was killed soon after this visit, at the Battle of Lincoln, where the French army suffered great losses, so: 'deprived of help for the present, despairing of the future and being pressed by imminent starvation, made peace with the legate [the Pope's representative] and King's supporters . . . Surrendered . . . the City of London and all the castle . . . . . . [and Louis] returned to France with his men'.

More Trouble in Dunstable

The Priory annalist has a very long entry for the year 1220; it includes a brief, unemotional sentence concerning the danger that Dunstable and vicinity were suffering from the castles at

Luton and Eaton Bray. No doubt soldiers from both castles were buying, with or without ready money, food from the market and also from commercial and even private storerooms. If they had clashed, there would have been fighting and bystanders could have been hurt or killed.

In Bedfordshire 'peace' was still not very peaceful! William Marshall in 1219 failed to get the Manor of Luton back. Falkes built his small, motte and bailey castle in the area between St. Mary's church and the River Lea; his builders quite ruthlessly knocked down houses, flooded others, blocked a road and, to fill the moat, diverted the River Lea, flooding the church fields and preventing the church mill from working.

Kidnap at Dunstable

In 1223, the people of Luton took their complaints to the king's judges when they visited Bedford, but Falkes refused to attend. Since 1211 or before, Falkes had been a loyal and brave soldier and despite all the complaints Henry was slow to interfere. Then he was suspected of being involved in a conspiracy in Wales and of being friendly with the king's enemies. Although during Christmas 1223/4 he went with others to Northampton and surrendered his castles and royal honours, he held on to Bedford and Luton and again refused to attend. However, when the damaged Lutonians took their grievances back to Bedford the judges sent an official message that he must attend their next court at Dunstable Priory, or be sent into exile. The three judges arrived and thirty-two people from Luton made their claims, mainly of stolen land, e.g. Roger de Ho accused Falkes of taking thirty acres from his father; also the representative from St. Albans Abbey described their grievances concerning the mill[1]. Falkes was found guilty on all charges, heavily fined and it was recommended that he should be outlawed. Then to everyone's horror, a messenger arrived to say that Falkes' brother, William and a group of soldiers, had ridden out from Bedford Castle, to kidnap the judges! News reached Dunstable

---

1   B.H.R.S. Vol. IX.

in time for them to escape, in different directions; two of them
got away but Henry de Brayboc rode straight into a trap and
was carried off to Bedford Castle. His wife, Christiana, and her
escort rode to Northampton to beg the King for help and this
time Falkes had gone too far. When summoned to attend the
King he escaped to the estates of his friend, the Earl of Chester,
on the Welsh border and when Henry realised that Falkes had
slipped away he issued orders that Bedford Castle should be
surrounded and he began to plan for a major siege.

Preparations for a Siege

Without waiting to finalise his plans the King set off south with
his church leaders, Chief Justice and those barons who were
with him, including William Marshall and William de
Cantilupe. No doubt William de Beauchamp was consulted
about strategic points concerning the castle's defence although
his presence is not recorded at Northampton. Henry was only
sixteen years old but he had grown up with soldiers, and sieges
were to him a familiar form of warfare. He and his advisors
made plans as they rode and by the time that they stopped for
the night at Newport Pagnell Henry was ready to send off
messages in all directions. These 'messages' were royal
commands and were to be obeyed 'in haste' or 'without delay'.

A siege was a slow operation and Henry prepared for a long
wait; a royal tent was to be sent from London and thirty casks of
wine. The cooks might be able to use locally produced food
supplemented with almonds, spice and ginger from the royal
stillroom, but the wine which was to be provided from
Northampton might not be good enough for use in the royal tent!
Although he had sent for his sporting dogs, this was not going to
be a country picnic where the attackers sat feasting until the castle
starved; Brayboc and the other prisoners must be released
quickly. Many of the weapons were too big to transport, so their
construction was allowed for on site. From Newport, messages
were sent out ordering the local sheriffs to provide hides for
making slings, cords and cables to work the engines and also
slings to 'throw' large blocks of stone by using a winch. The

Sheriff of London was to send wax to grease the cords. The monks at Newnham (near Bedford) were to provide 'rawstone' to be made into shot and the Sheriff of Bedfordshire was to send for quarrymen and masons (from Totternhoe?) to come with their tools to work the stone into shot. Smaller weapons could be transported, so at the Tower of London smiths were to work day and night making crossbows for immediate use and others were to be transported from distant Corfe Castle.

The account of the battle in the Dunstable Priory Annals describes the use of mangonels. They had to be set up some distance from the castle and to the horror of the local people, the church leaders stood by and allowed the engineers to take down the towers of St. Paul's and St. Cuthbert's churches!

The letters went out from Newport on Thursday 20th June; at Bedford, on three successive days, a group of military and church leaders, including the Prior of Newnham, had demanded, in the king's name, the surrender of the castle. William de Breauté had defied them saying it was his brother's castle and that the King could not demand entry. When messengers told Henry this he swore to hang them all! The Archbishop of Canterbury arrived and on June 20th read the solemn service of excommunication on all who held the castle against the king. On June 21st the King arrived at Bedford and the siege officially began. When, many weeks later, it was decided to make a major attack, 'the men of Dunstable', who had suffered so greatly from Falkes and his soldiers and suffered the indignity of the kidnap, were allowed (a doubtful honour?) to lead the attack. Their account is so clear that it is possible that one or more of the canons were present.

The Siege of Bedford Castle
From a new translation of the Annals of Dunstable Priory by Mrs Elizabeth North.

'Page 90 –
In the same year on the eighth day after Pentcost (June 9) the justices itinerant were at Dunstable. There Fawkes was

convicted of thirty-five seisins. He was so infuriated that when
the justiciars were leaving, he set an ambush, then on his
instructions Henry Braybrook was seized and many troubles
resulted from this.

Page 87 –
Meanwhile, however, Fawkes withdrew and stayed in the Earl
of Chester's land, when the destruction of the castle was
imminent . . . Fawkes [travelled] to Northampton. While he was
there with King's safe conduct and Martin of Pateshull and the
Archdeacon of Bedford* were conducting peace negotiations
between him and the King, the castle was captured in this way.
On the east there was one petrary and two mangonels which
attacked the tower every day. On the west side there were two
mangonels which battered the old tower. And there was one
mangonel on the south and one on the north which made two

A wooden tower erected to help soldiers break into a defended castle. O.R.

---

* John Houghton.

entrances in the walls nearest them. Besides these, there were two wooden towers made by a carpenter raised above the top of the tower and castle for the use of crossbowmen and spies. In addition to these there were several engines in which both crossbowmen and slingers hid in ambush. In addition there was a seige-engine called the Cat, beneath which underground diggers called miners could go in and out while they undermined the walls of the tower and castle. However, the castle was taken in four assaults. In the first the barbican was captured where four or five outsiders were killed. In the second the outer bailey was captured, where several were killed and our men acquired horses with harness, breastplates, crossbows, oxen, bacon and live pigs and countless other plunder.

Page 88 –
However they burnt the outhouses with the corn and hay which were inside. In the third assault a wall near the old keep fell because of the action of miners and our men entered there and seized the inner bailey in the face of great danger. In this occupation many of our men perished. Ten of our men, too, wishing to enter the keep, were shut in and held by the enemy. But at the fourth assault, on the Eve of Assumption, about the time of vespers, miners set fire to the keep so that smoke poured into the room in the keep where the enemy were; the keep cracked with the result that fissures appeared in its side. Then since the enemy despaired of their safety, Fawkes' wife and all the women with her, and Henry, the King's justiciar, with the other knights who had previously been imprisoned, were allowed to leave safe and sound and the enemy subjected themselves to the King's commands, hoisting his standard at the top of the keep, thus they remained under royal guard in the keep that night. But the following morning, they were brought before the King's tribunal and absolved from excommunication by the bishops: more than eighty were hanged on the instructions of the King and justiciar. But the King pardoned three for the Templars on the pleas of the bishops, so that they might fight in the Holy Land in their habit.

The castle chaplain was handed over to the archbishop to be judged in an ecclesiastical court. It is not easy to describe how much treasure, how many weapons and supplies were found in the keep. Thus all the men Fawkes had in England dispersed without moveable or immoveable goods.

After these events, however, Fawkes was taken to Bedford with a small escort. His men were absolved but he remained under pain of punishment until he should restore to the King the Castle of Plympton, the castle of Stokes-Curci, gold and silver vessels, and the money which he had, thus he was brought to London.

Meanwhile a sheriff was ordered to destroy the keep and outer bailey, but the inner bailey remained for William Beauchamp to live in after the removal of the battlements and the filling in of the ditches on all sides. However, the stone was granted to the canons of Newnham and Cauldwell and the church of St. Paul at Bedford. Afterwards, Fawkes was absolved in London and because he taken the cross he was allowed to leave for Rome . . . [He had many adventures and appealed to both the King and the Pope for help] . . . Thus burdened by many debts, returning from Rome, he died at St. Ciriac'.

The End of the Story

So except for Falkes de Breauté, who was exiled and died abroad, the baddies were hung and the damage that they did to the people of Dunstable, Luton and round about was eventually forgotten.

William Marshall and William Beauchamp both got their estates back but the castles were destroyed. The Bedford churches, which had been damaged, were recompensed and although there is no record of official compensation for the people of Luton, they may well have been with the Dunstablians and shared in the spoil taken during the fighting to break the siege.

Chapter 7

The Town v The Priory
– 1220 to 1230

When King Henry I founded Dunstable he promised the burgesses who came to live in his new town the privileges accorded to the burgesses of London. The charter drawn up when Henry gave the town to the Priory not only gave the Prior control of the market by 'sac and soc', but also the right to hold a court and administer fines and 'suits, services and customs', which meant the burgesses were obliged to attend his court, pay money rent and, when required to do so, had also to work on the Priory farms[1]. These two statements were contradictory and unless very tactfully and skillfully handled would lead to trouble. Villagers, used to the feudal system, accepted compulsory attendance at the lord's court every two or three weeks but the burgesses were often away at markets in other towns and would receive constant fines for their absence.

Trouble Concerning Tithes
Above is an example of a secular disagreement but in addition, there was the problem of tithes. Everyone involved in farming knew that they had to give one-tenth of everything they grew, or made, to the church. The Prior, as their spiritual leader, demanded from the burgesses one-tenth profit from all business, 'wherever it was carried on'. This was because so much of the farming part of their work was carried out at

---

1   For examples of work service demanded by the Priory, from their tenants at Houghton, see B.H.R.S. Vol. IXX – The Treatise of the Priory.

Caddington and Kensworth and their financial business in London and elsewhere.

Work Service
Richard de Morins was elected Prior in 1202. He was respected by the bishops, the King and the Pope but he seems to have been insensitive in dealing with the burgesses. Below are examples, mainly taken from the charters, which pinpoint the disagreements which developed between de Morins and the burgesses.

Although the burgesses were 'free' men, much of their property, owned by the Priory, carried work service. John Young had such a farmhouse in which he had a tenant but John was the Prior's tenant (in chief); the Prior demanded service, John ignored him and the Prior impounded John's cattle![1]

365. Each village elected a reeve to act as foreman; the Prior had a reeve to be his spokesman/messenger/representative. When Ralph Young was elected (he was a business-man; often away from the town; his time was money!), he refused to do it and was fined £2.

362. In a list of tenants who had done a day's service as reapers were included the King's coroner, a goldsmith and other burgesses, but they would not have worked in the harvest fields themselves, instead sending one of their own labourers.

The Young Family
The serious trouble started in 1220, when the Annals record '. . . the Prior obtained tithes of hay against many parishioners . . .'[2]. The parishioners were not against the church or the Priory, only against the unsympathetic attitude of the Prior. Taking the Young family who were one of the families who led the fight for freedom, as an example, Alexander gave twelve houses and four shops to the Priory, and Richard and

---

1   B.H.R.S. Vol. III, p.304.
2   Although the Annals printed in the Rolls Series are in Latin, the section covering this period has been translated by the staff of the County Record Office, to whom I am very grateful. CRT/170/1/9.

Ralph gave the sacristan lights to burn in honour of the Blessed Virgin Mary, during the period of the troubles. Yet Charter 451 records that in 1221, John, Archdeacon of Bedford had settled a dispute between Alexander and John Young concerning tithes of the windmill, and against Richard son of John concerning tithes of hay, and against all three plus William son of William, tithes of trade[1].

So bitter was the dispute concerning tithes, that the Prior had appealed to the Pope, who had asked the Abbot of Warden Abbey to set up an enquiry. Meanwhile the Bishop of Lincoln had asked the local archdeacon to investigate a dispute concerning customs and offerings. These matters were settled and for a time there was peace, but the Young family were in trouble again in 1225. John and Alexander took possession of inherited property without paying the Prior for a 'licence' or death duty. He took them to court and they were fined. Yet that was the year Alexander made his generous gift of property; one would have thought they could have settled the matter out of court. John was also in trouble for not paying his tithes.

Trying to trace a pattern of events from a few legal statements is of course dangerous, but this seems to illustrate the different attitudes to the Priory in general and to the Prior in particular.

A Fight in the High Street
Things quietened down until 1227 when Henry III demanded £100 to renew the Prior's charter. Despite its restrictions, the presence of the Priory gave the burgesses advantages in their business affairs, so the Prior demanded that they should pay two-thirds. The bailiff went round collecting but Martin Duke refused to pay. We do not know why, perhaps he was ill or in trouble but he had the support of the burgesses and does not appear himself in the resulting fracas. The bailiff claimed Duke's uncut corn in lieu of money, so John Young

---

1   B.H.R.S. Vol. X.

decided to cut it and take it to a place of safety. 'An affray' started between the servants of the Prior and the burgesses, and men from both sides were wounded. Victory was won by the Prior's household when a cart, belonging to Alexander Young, half-full of the aforesaid wheat, was brought safely into the Prior's court 'in spite of their adversaries'[1]. Traffic in Dunstable must have been brought to a standstill while the Young family's servants fought in the middle of the High Street to stop the Prior's servants from getting the cart through the gateway and into the Great Courtyard, now the Priory Gardens. Judging from the number of people involved, it was quite a fight!

When the Prior set up a court of enquiry as to who started the fight, John Flitton accused Henry Duke, John Young and certain others. Henry Duke accused John of Daceby (Leics.) and John of Flitton, both of whom were connected with the Priory. So the Prior took the whole matter to the King's travelling judges. In their enthusiasm, men on the same side denied each other's evidence and the judges were utterly confused and refused to pass judgement.

The Burgesses Revolt

This incident seems to have united the burgesses and they rose against the Prior. There is a suggestion in the Annals of 1226, that the burgesses tried to hold their own court but in 1227 '. . . when we had the mayorality of the town of Dunstable in our hands, a quarrel arose between ourselves and the townsmen about fines for offences'.

The King's Judges Were Consulted

Traditionally, the fine had been 4d. (1⅔p), for all crimes. The Prior had raised it without consulting the town. For this and other matters the burgesses sued him when the judges came to Bedford in November[2]. They had five main complaints:

---

1   Annals 1227.
2   Fully reported B.H.R.S. Vol. X, 304 and 277.

1. The taking of John Young's cows when they were out in the lane, away from the farmhouse where the dispute lay.
2. The Prior had on one occasion held his court in London and still insisted that they attend, so they had lost time and money.
3. When some of them had been arrested, outside of Dunstable, and wrongly accused, they had been put in Bedford prison; he did not stand bail for them.
4. For another Bedford court hearing he had sent someone round door-to-door and demanded the whole town should attend, when all that was necessary was the reeve and twelve burgesses.
5. The matter of fines; 4d. being what they had paid 'in the time of Henry the Elder [I] and before the church of Dunstable had been founded, and constantly thereafter, until the priory vexed them thereon'.*

Then it was the Prior's turn, his spokesman said:

1. John's cows were in the lane belonging to the offending house and anyway he owned the whole town.
2. He denied making them go to London but merely suggested they should go for arbitration.
3. He had refused to bail them out of Bedford because they had claimed privileges he did not agree with, so he had not interfered.

In each case the judges ruled for the Prior and the townsmen were fined. The Prior seemed to be getting it all his own way, especially as in answer to Clause 4, they had to agree that originally the Prior sent the reeve to ask only twelve of them to go to Bedford but so many of them could not go and sent replacements that it got confused and so everyone was

---

* In addition, Elicia, widow of Ralph Young, claimed her dower, which she had been refused at the Prior's Court; the judge refused to discuss it while the other trial was on.

summoned. Then came Clause 5, the altering of customs given by Henry to the burgesses, before he gave their freedom to the Prior.

Both sides put their case but the royal connection made it too political for the judges, who refrained from comment and sent the case to the King's Court at Westminster.

This meant a long wait and there must have been ill feeling in the town meanwhile. During 1228, ten of the burgesses withheld their offerings at funerals and weddings and only two guests attended. The Prior excommunicated the ten ringleaders but they had so much support in the town that they went to the altar amongst their friends and for some time were not recognised! When the Prior did realise what was happening he closed the church and, from August 1st until October 9th, no services were held in the Priory Church, the canons attending mass in their infirmary chapel.

The Bishop of Lincoln Visits the Priory
The Bishop of Lincoln (who must have been quite desperate) came to Dunstable and from the pulpit solemnly excommunicated the ten and their friends. However on the very same day the Archdeacon of Bedford, John of Houghton, who may have known the men and understood their complaints, together with his colleague of Lincoln, negotiated a settlement. The burgesses were to be 'absolved according to the form of the church'. In return for which the Prior demanded £20 but the mediators reduced it by a third.

King Henry III Intervenes
When King Henry III passed through Dunstable in 1229 and lodged at the Priory, the Prior asked him to rule on the outstanding legal battle. The King consulted his council and made a settlement which at the time and in the presence of the King was accepted by the leading burgesses. However, once the King had departed, they ignored it.

The Prior sent messengers to inform the King, who got the sheriff to send 'twelve lawful and discreet men' to represent the town at his court at Westminster. The judges decided to agree with the King's verdict and the sheriff was instructed to see that it was carried out. Briefly, if the King taxed burgesses on other royal estates (tallage) the Prior could tax the town. On the other hand, fines should be kept at 4d. plus 'the making of amends'. This allowed the Prior to fix high 'injury' money if anyone from the Priory was wounded (presumably legally as well as physically). With regards to attending court, they need not attend unless personally involved; nor need they attend if they were away on business, or if they were ill.

Even the special court, which once each year had to be attended by everyone over fifteen years old, could be missed if they were 'at remote parts', 'at fairs', or 'across the sea'. Also, they must be given one month's warning of the date. As in the past the absentees had regularly been fined, this must have been a serious cause of annoyance amongst the travelling burgesses and it is surprising that an educated, experienced man like Richard de Morins had not made terms like these years ago.

The Price of Bread and Beer

It wasn't long before a new dispute broke out, 'the assize of bread and wine'. As Lord of the Manor, the Prior fixed the price of retail sales, depending on the cost of raw materials (e.g. the success of the harvest). The ruling was that if bakers or brewers overcharged they would be fined 4d. (1⅔p) the first and second time, but for the third offence the Prior would take all their stock for his own use. For any fourth and subsequent offences 'the wrong-doer shall undergo punishment by the tumbril and pillory and none the less the Prior shall have the bread and beer'!

Another Tax

It was the tallage, essentially a royal tax, which particularly infuriated the burgesses and they refused to pay unless they were ordered to do so by the King. So the King wrote to the sheriff '. . . we charge you see to it that the said Prior tallages the burgesses in a reasonable manner . . .'. The unfortunate sheriff came to collect the tax but was refused by most of the people that he approached. The townspeople held that the command only applied to the Prior's tenants in chief; those burgesses who held property direct from the Prior. The sheriff consulted the king, who agreed, and the Prior, 'whose plans had been upset by these letters' called in twelve burgesses he thought he could trust to collect from the tenants in chief. 'They took a corporal oath that they would assess the tallage reasonably that they would not burden their fee unjustly, nor spare their friends . . .'.

In fact, they collected only sixty-three shillings as the wealthy men of the town had only been assessed at three shillings each. The Prior made this known and the people rose in fury and withdrew their tithes and offerings and only offered 1d. at family ceremonies – and so it went on.

Peace at Last

Charter 361 is the agreement which was finally reached in 1230, based on the previous ruling of the king. The burgesses were to pay £60 in return for which there would be no more tallage[1].

Unfortunately, we do not know how much tallage had been demanded or how soon there would have been a new demand. Sixty pounds was a great deal of money in 1230, but in 1227 Henry III had demanded £100 and so a once and for all payment of £60 was probably good value. At least it brought peace to the town.

---

1   B.H.R.S. Vol. X.

Chapter 8

The Peasants' Revolt
– 1381

Working Together

At the height of their quarrel with Richard de Morins, the burgesses negotiated with William de Cantilupe, Lord of the Manor of Eaton Bray, to move their business centre onto forty acres of his land, where they would be free of the Prior's tolls and taxes.

However, once the subject of the Prior's tolls was finally settled, things quietened down and the burgesses worked together with successive priors to make Dunstable an even more successful town. At first corn and leather seem to have been the chief raw materials with which they traded, but later they took full advantage of the expanding wool market. In addition to this their own domestic market was financially important and most of the residents, poor and rich, benefitted by the pilgrims and other travellers attracted to the town by the presence of the Priory.

After the death of Prior Richard de Morins, in 1242, when there followed a period of bad weather, lost harvests and great poverty, the priors were often in debt and became dependent on the richer burgesses for help. These priors may have been less autocratic than de Morins. Undoubtedly there were disputes from time-to-time but the next major quarrel seems not have been until 1381, when the burgesses took advantage of the national – so called – Peasants' Revolt to try and win their complete freedom.

The Poll Tax and Other Causes

This is not the place to discuss the reasons for the revolt for not only are they extremely complex but in part varied from county to county. Issues came to a head, like the introduction of a poll tax, which after many years of a tax, more like our system of rates, seemed bitterly unfair and affected the whole country. Some of the people from Kent who marched to London, to meet the boy king, Richard II, may have done so because of this tax.

The wealthy burgesses of Dunstable were less likely to have been more seriously upset by the poll tax than by the religious issues. We shall find in the second book in this series that in later centuries the people of Dunstable became leaders in the struggle to get freedom of worship. The burgesses of St. Albans were in much the same position as those of Dunstable and nearly all the local people who joined in the great revolt came from towns and villages where they had been dominated by the officials of religious houses. So when the men of Kent marched north into London, they met people from Bury St. Edmunds, Ely, Cambridge and several other such places who were demanding both secular and to a lesser extent religious freedom. People from Barnet are said to have told the burgesses of St. Albans what was happening in London and so a large crowd from that town then hurried to join those who had already arrived in London. Wildly excited they returned to St. Albans, where a great deal of damage was done to Abbey property, mainly against people, buildings and documents which were thought to be connected with the administration of rents and taxes. The sub-cellarer's house, the Abbey prison, the offices, the rabbit warrens and other reserves, where farmers were prevented from snaring and hunting on their own land, were all attacked.

This was Friday 14th and Saturday 15th June 1381. Men and women from all the towns and villages round about, wherever the Abbey held land, poured into the town and joined in the confusion. Saturday being market day, traders from Dunstable joined the throng and were there in time to witness the arrival of a group who had returned with a charter, signed by the fourteen year old King, telling the Abbot to hand over the old, contentious documents and to negotiate new terms. To disperse the dangerously large crowds which were threatening London, the young King had signed many such charters. This one requested the Abbot to hand over the various charters that affected the townspeople. At that point of extreme excitement, the Dunstable traders left the town and rode back to Dunstable as fast as they could go. Had they waited until the early hours of Sunday morning, they would have known that royal knights arrived to proclaim the King's peace.

However, backed by men from towns and villages round about, armed with bows, pitchforks and stones, the burgesses of St. Albans stood firm and eventually received a new charter. All was reasonably peaceful until the end of the month, then law enforcement officers, backed by the King, began to make secret arrests and village by village the people began to sue for pardons. The King and his judges arrived on Friday, July 12th and as the revolt was completely squashed, horrendous punishments were awarded. Many of the men from St. Albans and some from the towns and villages round about were imprisoned and several national leaders were hung, drawn and quartered.

The Revolt in Dunstable

Thanks to Prior Thomas Marshall nothing horrific like this happened in Dunstable; an account of the events, after the traders returned to the town, has been recorded in the Annals of the Priory. It starts with a short account of what had happened in St. Albans, then continues:

'Some of our traders were that day at St. Albans market, and saw it all, and laid the same design, and came to us a little before vespers. The first executor of their malice, Thomas Hobbes, the worthless mayor [leading burgess] of Dunstable, falsely accosted as from the King, Thomas Marshall the Prior, whom he had never spoken to, who returned it by putting off his hood, and bowing his head, demanded the King's pleasure. Hobbes, in an insolent manner, told him it was that he should grant the townspeople a Charter of Liberty as they had from Henry I.

At first the Prior refused; but reflecting on what had happened at London and St. Albans, yielded so far to the mob and the request of the townsmen, as to grant them a charter, sealed with our common seal. At that time William Croyser, Kt., and William Bateman had sheltered themselves among us from the mob, and advised us to comply with all they asked; and we inserted in the charter that they should do fealty to the Prior. But this forced grant did not last long for the mob could not agree among themselves about the article excluding the neighbouring butchers and fishmongers from selling their goods here. At last, however, it was sealed.

Soon after, the King having got the better of the insurrections, punished them as they deserved, and did the same at St. Albans where John Ball, the priest, was hanged and quartered.

The Prior, watching his opportunity, first endeavoured by fair words to get the charter back. But when this would not do, he summoned them to St. Albans, and got it cancelled as being extorted by force. He was at great expense and risk to deliver his townsmen. While the rest of the nobility revenged themselves entirely or in part, by bloodshed, he alone in these parts exposed his life and property in defence of his trust.'

Prior Thomas Marshall, as recorded by the annalist, '. . . was at great expense and risk to deliver his townsmen'. This means that although he had to summon the leading burgesses to the king's court in St. Albans before he got his charters back, he then had to speak up for them and possibly even distribute bribes to prevent them coming to the same ghastly end as the leaders in St. Albans[1].

From the next reference to Thomas Hobbes (see below) we learn that he was landlord of the Swan Inn (later the Red Lion) on the corner of North Street and East Street.

---

1   The account of the revolt in St. Albans is printed in The Rolls Series, 'The Abbey Chroniclers'. The account is in English.

Chapter 9

Royal Visitors to Dunstable
– 1131 to 1341

Placed as Dunstable was, less than forty miles from London and on the direct routes to Wales, to the north and to northwest England, many royal parties broke their journeys there. Because of this Dunstable became associated with several important historical events.

Council at Northampton
It is possible that Henry I and his courtiers stayed in Dunstable during 1131, on their way to Northampton. On November 25th, 1120, both Henry's legitimate sons had been drowned at sea, leaving the succession very insecure. He still had a favourite illegitimate son, Robert, Earl of Gloucester, and a daughter, Matilda, who was married to Geoffrey, Count of Anjou, but would the people of England accept either of them? So in 1131 he ordered all his barons and church leaders to meet him at the church of The Holy Sepulchre, Northampton, where after some discussion they swore an oath to accept Matilda, and Henry relied on her half brother to support her claim.

Council at Dunstable
However, when Henry died in Normandy in 1135, both Matilda and Earl Robert were with him, and so Henry's nephew, Stephen who was in England was crowned instead of Matilda.

During the next ten years England suffered a civil war, as first Earl Robert and then Matilda's son supported her. The barons wanted to end the fighting; a truce was arranged and as

Stephen had held his Christmas court at Kingsbury, in 1136, and knew how convenient it was, a peace conference was arranged there in 1154. Stephen, Henry and their advisors met to make plans to end the fighting and for Henry (Matilda's son) to become heir to Stephen's throne[1]. He was crowned King Henry II the following year.

King John gives Kingsbury to the Priory

Henry's son, John, made several visits to Dunstable but he must have decided that Kingsbury was too expensive to maintain, just for occasional visits. When he visited in 1204 he gave to the Priory 'the site and garden' where King Henry I 'once had houses'. He said they could use them to build for themselves as they pleased.

King Henry III Makes Gifts to the Priory

The Dunstable Annals are polite about the royal visits but the true picture is shown by Matthew Paris of St. Albans who wrote about Henry III: 'He sought his lodgings and his meals with abbots, priors, clerks and men of low degree, staying with them and asking for gifts . . . nay, the Queen herself did not blush to ask for them' [gifts] 'not as a favour but as her due . . .'. No wonder there are references in the Annals to the Priory being in debt!

Henry III and Queen Eleanor made several visits to the Priory and although on one occasion they gave silk cloths and one hundred shillings in silver, the Prior in return gave them each a gilt cup and Princess Margaret and Prince Edward received a gold buckle. In 1254 the Priory sent King Henry III a cup of silver gilt worth 100 shillings.

King Edward I Leads a Funeral Procession

The Priory also had the expense of entertaining Henry's son, Edward and his Queen, Eleanor. Although Henry had at one time sent a silver cup to the Priory, to carry the communion

---

1   J.T.Appleby. The Troubled Reign of King Stephen. The date 1137 recorded by Worthington Smith comes from the old calendar.

wine to the poor vagrants sleeping rough around the town and although Edward paid for his visit with a valuable altar cloth, neither gift replaced the food eaten by the large parties.

One of the most important royal visits was that which followed the death of Queen Eleanor on November 28th 1290. The royal party was heading north when the Queen became ill. She rested at the house of Richard Weston at Hardby, near Lincoln, but became worse and then died. On December 4th the funeral procession left for London[1]. They chose a route which would enable them to visit all the religious houses on the way.

When they arrived at Dunstable, on December 12th, the coffin was placed on a suitable table near the crossroads so that the people might pay homage. The coffin was then carried into the Priory for the night, where it was watched over by the canons; the next morning the procession moved on to St. Albans. To mark the occasion the Priory received two precious cloths and about 120lbs of wax for replacing the candles which would have been burnt around the coffin, throughout the night. Later King Edward decided to build an elaborate cross at each site where the coffin had rested. The Annals record the planning of the Dunstable cross in 1290 but the payment, of just over £100, is entered in the Pipe Rolls for 1310/11. John of Battle supervised the building of crosses at Northampton, Stony Stratford, Woburn, Dunstable and St. Albans. The Northampton cross is still standing; it is decorated with a carving of Queen Eleanor and other figures which were once embellished by the work of William Torel, a London goldsmith. On the 700th anniversary, in 1990, a commemorative service was held in Westminster Abbey and a group from Dunstable took part.

The cross is mentioned in rent lists and sale documents; e.g. in a deed dated 1542, when John Dyve sold the Swan Inn (later the Red Lion) to Roger Parkyns it was described as standing in the North Street of Dunstable, in front of the high cross. Lambourne in 1803 and Worthington Smith both mention the

1   J.Powrie, 'Eleanor of Castile'. Published by Brewin Books, in 1986.
      This covers the history of the Eleanor Crosses.

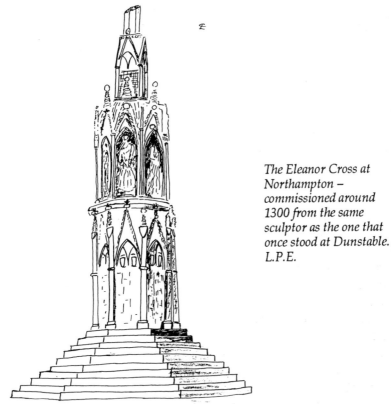

The Eleanor Cross at Northampton – commissioned around 1300 from the same sculptor as the one that once stood at Dunstable. L.P.E.

foundations of the cross being uncovered on High Street North, outside the Nags Head, but it probably stood in the middle of the crossroads.

In 1985 builders Robinson and White commissioned sculptress Miss Dora Barrett to design and make a statue for the nearby Queen Eleanor precinct. Dunstable Town Council have commemorated the procession, with a plaque on the wall of the National Westminster Bank.

Kingsbury Palace

Unfortunately very little is known about Kingsbury during the period that it was owned by the Priory, although there is a reference to Henry IV staying at 'the old royal palace, Dunstable' on November 3rd 1405, when he was travelling

*Modern Queen Eleanor
statue, sculpted by
Dora Barret, 1986.
L.P.E.*

back to London after fighting in Wales[1]. Later, on December
3rd 1408, he again stayed in Dunstable when he was on a
journey from Berkhamsted Castle to Daventry[2]. It is possible
that the 'palace' had been divided up into two or three separate
houses and that the canons let them out to one or more of the
wealthier burgesses. In 1329, when King Edward III had
brought such a large party to the Dunstable tournament that
there had been too many for the Prior's guest house and hostel,
it was decided to repair the house of 'the late John Durrant' to
house the overflow. Seven carpenters, six tilers and two
plasterers worked for nine days and used 1,000 tiles, 1,000
lathes and over 4,000 nails; they probably put on a new roof[3].

1   Wylie – History of England Under Henry IV – Vol. II.
2   Op.cit. Vol. III.
3   V.C.H. Vol. III.

There is no reference to name 'Kingsbury' but that is quite likely the building which they used. John Durrant had had several business interests. He had been a sheep farmer trading locally and in distant places. He was one of the richest men in Bedfordshire and had been very generous to the Priory.

Tournaments

Placed as it was on the crossing of two main roads and not too far from London, Dunstable was often chosen for tournaments. Where they were held we do not know, though the whole town only covered about 400 acres. Some of these tournaments were no more than jousts between two men but some were much bigger. After the Battle of Lewes, the Earl of Gloucester and 'a large party of men' came to Dunstable to 'fight' against the sons of Simon de Montfort and their supporters. King Henry III forbade it but it wasn't called off until Simon de Montfort arrived in the town.

When Edward II came to a tournament in 1309, there were 235 knights and squires taking part and each one of them would have had supporters, servants and grooms. A great deal of space would have been needed for tented accommodation. Of the four corners of Dunstable there was no room on the two which backed on to Houghton Regis. The space may have overflowed, out of Dunstable, along the foot of Blows Downs, across the present golf course on top of Dunstable Downs or in the present cemetery – Catch Acre area, which was the boundary with Kensworth.

On several other occasions Dunstable was chosen as a venue by certain noblemen because it was sufficiently far from London for plotting and planning against the king, and on more than one occasion messengers arrived just in time to forbid the meetings, in the king's name, and to order the knights to return home.

One of the biggest tournaments was in 1341, when Dunstable may have been chosen in honour of Sir Nigel Loring of Chalgrave, (thought to be the model for the White Knight of Conan Doyle's adventure stories). He had been the hero of a naval battle at the port of Sluys, knighted for his bravery, and sent back to England with the news of victory. This tournament was possibly the last to be held in the town. King Edward III and Queen Phillipa were there with all the 'great people of England' including Maud of Lancaster, Lady of the manor of Leighton, and her brother, soon to become the Earl of Lancaster. She gave him five quarters of wheat to help with his expenses at the tournament[1]. It would be interesting to know if his steward sold the wheat in Dunstable market or if he made a gift of it to the Priory.

The royal tournaments especially drew large crowds. The presence of so many wealthy people must have brought a great deal of money into the town and the itinerant vendors and entertainers who followed them would have brought excitement, but the rowdiness, drunkenness, pick-pockets and thieves were not so welcome!

---

1   B.H.R.S. Vol. III, p.21.

Chapter 10

Dunstable in the Fifteenth and Sixteenth Centuries

Life Around the Crossroads

The advantages for the people of Dunstable of living around an important crossroads was that the Priory and numerous inns attracted a great number of travellers, which resulted in a high level of employment and general prosperity. The situation also encouraged commuting London businessmen to settle, leading to more jobs. The constant coming and going of travellers gave the opportunity to over-hear, in the inns and stables, all the latest news and gossip.

The disadvantages were that some of the travellers were not so welcome. There were those who were not as honest as they should have been and others brought infectious diseases. One of the more serious problems was that caused by soldiers on the march, who either slept in tents outside the town or who were compulsorily billeted in the town. They often arrived short of supplies, and not having been paid for several weeks would, during their stay, carry out thefts and do damage.

Queen Margaret of Anjou Visits Dunstable

In 1461 Margaret, wife of the ailing king Henry VI, travelling south, towards what would become known as the Second Battle of St. Albans, tried a manoeuvre to catch the Yorkist soldiers unprepared. She branched west and then east and approached St. Albans along the Watling Street, instead of from the north. Her soldiers, who were reported to have been very hungry and out of the control of their officers, camped in Dunstable both before and after the battle. It must have been very frightening for the residents of Dunstable, for whilst their first visit was quite short, on their return, after winning the battle, they stayed for some time, while Queen Margaret negotiated with officials of the City of London, who would not let her wild and unruly soldiers enter the city.

It may have been before or after that battle that a valuable brooch was lost or deposited in the town.

The Dunstable Gold Swan Brooch

One of Dunstable's greatest treasures, this brooch is on show in the display of Medieval jewellery, at the British Museum. So specialised is the design and construction of the brooch that, although frustratingly we have no real knowledge as to how it came to Dunstable, experts have been able to tell us quite a lot about the brooch itself. Not only is the 'Dunstable Swan Jewel', as the British Museum has called it, part of the town's history but its discovery and the way that it came to be in the museum is also of great interest.

Finding The Brooch. In 1965 the Manshead Archaeological Society was excavating in Friary Field, Dunstable, the known site of a Dominican Friary (Grid ref. TL 019217). It was a warm

The Dunstable Swan Jewel. B.M.

82

dry summer and the excavation was extremely interesting. These combined factors resulted in a high proportion of the Manshead Society turning out to dig each Sunday morning and three evenings during the week.

In one corner of the field was a raised area, which could have been the church or some other exciting building but in fact it turned out to be a heap of rubbish! Nevertheless it was mediaeval rubbish associated with the Friary, and the Site Director, Mr C. L. Matthews, would often ask diggers to take a turn in the 'long cut' across the rubbish heap![1]

On Friday, July 16th, a group were digging in the long cut, when to quote the finder, Maxene Miller, 'I found what I thought was another tree root, and pulled it, but it turned out to be a chain with a heavy earth covered lump on the end, about the size of a two-shilling (10p) piece. I was holding a brooch in the shape of a swan.' Everyone gathered round and it was obvious that the brooch was solid gold!

The law is quite clear about the excavation of gold objects, so Mr Matthews took the find to Dunstable police station, where it was formally received and locked away. The police notified the coroner and in October 1965 he took evidence of the finding of the brooch. Mr John Cherry M.A., Assistant Keeper of the Department of British and Mediaeval Antiquities at the British Museum, gave evidence of its date and importance.

The points to be decided were whether or not the brooch was valuable and if possible, whether it had been lost or deliberately hidden. Objects which are considered to have been deliberately hidden are judged to be Treasure Trove and automatically belong to the Crown, the finder getting a reward. Usually, valuable things which are judged to be unintentionally lost become the property of the landowner and this was the case with the Gold Swan. The police formally handed it over to Mr J. B. Stevens, the owner of Friary Field.

It was decided after much consideration that an article of such importance should be on show to the general public. The

---

1   M.A.S. Vol. 16, 'Archaeology of the Friary Site', 1966.

Dunstable Gold Swan Brooch was put up for auction at Sotheby's in March 1966 and sold to the Metropolitan Museum of New York for £4,800. An export licence was refused and, thanks to grants from the National Arts Collection Fund, the Pilgrim Fund and the Worshipful Company of Goldsmiths, it was subsequently bought by the British Museum, where it is currently on display.

Craftsmanship of The Swan Jewel and Its Possible Date. I am grateful to Mr John Cherry M.A. for letting me quote from an article that he wrote for the Journal of the British Archaeological Association[1].

'The Jewel is moulded in gold in the round. It is 1¼" high and 1" long. The chain is 3¼" long. It is covered with white enamel on the head, body, wings and legs. There are traces of black enamel for the eyes and feet. The gold has been moulded into blobs on the head, wings and legs before being covered with enamel to give the effect of feathers. The surface of the gold was roughened to ensure that the enamel stayed on. The wing of the Swan was originally slightly raised, but at some time it has been pressed closely against the body of the Swan, damaging the enamel where the wing joins the body and on the wing itself. The beak is slightly open and the right leg raised; both appear to be intentional rather than accidental. Around the neck there is a gold coronet with six fleur-de-lys to which is attached a chain of thirty links ending in a ring. At the back, the surface of the enamel is smooth and the jewel still has the original pin and catch.

The jewel is of gold decorated with white enamel. This technique of covering gold with white enamel is one of the characteristic features of the rich, gold enamelled work produced for the Court of France and Burgundy at the end of the fourteenth and beginning of the fifteenth centuries. It appears to have replaced the technique of émail-en-basse-taille current in the earlier years of the second half of the fourteenth

---

1 'Swan Legends and History': J. Cherry, 'The Dunstable Swan Jewel', Journal of the British Archaeological Association, 1969.

century, and of which the Royal Gold Cup, produced about
1380, is a leading example. Ulrich Middeldorf writing about the
origins of "émail-sur-ronde-bosse" in 1960 notes that the use of
white enamel on gold is not mentioned until 1380.

Two German historians, Müller and Steingräber, suggest
that by 1420, it is less easy to speak of this technique as Parisian
work, and both the growing influence of Netherlandish art on
goldsmiths' work and the increasing importance of Burgundian
patronage indicates that by the mid-fifteenth century the
technique of white enamel en-ronde-bosse was perhaps less
popular. A date in the second half of the fifteenth century
would therefore seem unlikely.'[1]

The Dunstable Fraternity

By the mid 15th century there were a number of wealthy
businessmen living in the town, several of whom were
members of the London based Wool Staplers' Company.

In 1442 a group of these men, headed by Laurence Pygot
and Henry Martell, bought a licence from King Henry VI and
started a fraternity or brotherhood, based at the Priory Church
of St. Peter, to employ a priest to say prayers and masses for the
souls of members, to reduce the time they spent in purgatory.
They dedicated it to St. John the Baptist and had their own
altar, which still survives in the north aisle. From their annual
subscriptions and income from the land they were given, they
supported their own priest to pray for 'the state of the said
Kyng and the brothers and systers of the sayd Gyld'[2].

Not much is known about the activities of the fraternity
except that they supported an almonry to provide
accommodation for six poor travellers and four of their own
members who were in need of help. This was in West Street
and may have been a continuation of the almonry of St. John
the Baptist which was run by the Priory in earlier years.

They had a brotherhood house and a house for the chaplain,

---

1   See also A. R. Wagner, 'The Swan Badge and the Swan Knight'.
     Archaeologia (1850–1) and 1959.
2   J.E.Brown, 'Chantry Certificates for Bedfordshire'.

in West Street, at least eight other houses and twenty pieces of land, in and around Dunstable, Houghton and Caddington, some quite small but several of which were over ten acres. The total brought in around £10 per year.

The Fraternity Register was kept on an annual basis and recorded the membership. It had long been thought that this register was lost or destroyed at the time of the closing of the fraternities. However, in 1947 some pages were included in a sale catalogue published by Sotheby's. An appeal was launched and the pages for the years 1506–1508 and 1522–1541 were bought by a group, known as 'The Friends of Luton Museum' for £500. It is not known if a register was kept every year of whether these were the only pages.

The Register is a volume of eighty-three parchment leaves, with border of gold and with colours which are still bright after four hundred years. The elborate illumination includes miniatures of the presidents and wardens and their wives and of the brethren and sisters of the Fraternity. The borders are entwined with delicately painted flowers, the Tudor rose, the split pomegranate of Catherine of Aragon, the arms of Dunstable and of the presidents, and the figures of King Henry VIII and Queen Catherine at prayer. On every page appears the severed head of St. John and for 1534 a miniature of Herod's feast, with the head appearing as the main dish on the table. Among the lists of members are the names of important national and local figures as well as numerous well-known families.

It is doubtful if we will ever know what happened to it during the very long period that it was missing but for many years before the sale it is thought to have been in the library of Sir Thomas Phillipps, the vendor.

Each year begins on a new page with an introductory paragraph giving the names of the president and the two wardens, written in red. For 1526 there are two separate entries with a different set of officers; for 1536, 1537, 1538, 1539 and 1541, there is no initial entry with the names of president and wardens. In 1526 a 'beadell' heads the list of members, and in

1531–5 and 1540 the name of the beadle is added in the paragraph with those of the presidents and wardens.

The handwriting is rarely the same for two years in succession and often two or more hands appear in the entries of one year. On many pages throughout the book the initial capitals are missing. It seems likely that the gloriously coloured capitals, page decorations and illustrations were inserted once every one or two years by an itinerant craftsman.

The annulment of the marriage between King Henry VIII and Queen Catherine of Aragon, at the Priory, caused the clerk much embarrassment and difficulty. Normally the Queen's name would have been included in the register beside that of King Henry, but this was now forbidden. Their entry reads 'Pray for the prosperous preservacion of the moste noble and Royall Estate of oure soverayne lorde Kynge Henry the VIII and Quene . . . his quene and all their progenitors.'

The name of the Queen Catherine of Aragon has been erased as have the few words following – perhaps the Queen's Spanish title or the name of the Princess Mary.

Not only did the written word have to be changed but also numerous royal badges and emblems depicted on glass and other materials[1]. Antonia Fraser noted payments made to Galyon Hone, the king's glazier, for work at Ampthill and elsewhere, as he repeatedly replaced 'the old Queen's badges'. She pointed out that 'By his marital career, Henry VIII proved himself to be the glazier's friend'[2].

Unworldly individuals who failed to note the change of queen could be arrested on a charge of treason.

The Fayrey Pall

One of the treasures of the Victoria and Albert Museum and used by them as the centrepiece of their 1990 exhibition, The Art of Death, is the Fayrey Pall.

The Fayrey family were members of the fraternity. They owned property in Dunstable and John Fayrey was a member

1   H. Calvin, ed., The History of the King's Works, IV.
2   A. Fraser. The Six Wives of Henry VIII.

*Memorial Brass of Henry
and Agnes Fayrey,
c.1516 from a recent
brass rubbing. R.D.*

of the Mercers' Company in London. There used to be a brass
in the Priory Church commemorating the lives of John's
parents Henry and Agnes Fayrey; it is also in the Victoria and
Albert Museum.

The pall or coffin cover is made of a very rich embroidery.
the middle is gold thread and red velvet pile in two thicknesses
and was probably brought from Florence, towards the end of
the 15th century. The sides and ends, which are of dark purple
velvet with English embroidery in gold and silver thread and
coloured silks, are thought to have been made in England.

The embroidery includes several figures and the names
John, Mary, Henry and Agnes Fayrey and it has been suggested
that the pall was commissioned by the Fayrey family and used
by members of the fraternity, some of whom are also
represented in the embroidery.

*The Fayrey Funeral Pall, donated to the Fraternity of St. John the Baptist,
c.1505. J.L.*

When the fraternity was closed the pall was lost, but in 1891
it was returned into the care of the rector of the Priory Church
and for many years it was known as the 'best' pall and hired
out at 6d. (2½p).

When its value was appreciated in the present century, it
was displayed in the Priory Church, in a glass case, but
eventually the Parochial Church Council realised that it was at
risk and it was given to the Victoria and Albert Museum, where
it is on permanent loan.

Henry VIII Visits Dunstable

From the time that King John gave Kingsbury Palace to the
Priory, nearly all the kings and queens of England stayed at
the Prior's house, alongside the present Priory Church.
During the early years of their marriage, King Henry VIII
stayed there with his young Queen Catherine of Aragon but

then things went wrong and what had been a happy marriage came to an end. This was partly because of events long past and partly because Henry had fallen wildly in love with the young Anne Boleyn.

Henry and the young Catherine of Aragon. Early in November 1501 the then ten-year-old Prince Henry accompanied the fifteen-year-old Catherine of Aragon to her wedding in St. Paul's Cathedral where she married Henry's older brother, Arthur. Shortly afterwards the young couple rode off to Ludlow but in less than six months Henry and Catherine were together again – at Arthur's funeral. Within weeks Catherine's family sent messengers to the English Court suggesting she should marry Henry! A few days before his twelfth birthday they were formally betrothed, but due firstly to Henry's age and then to political manoeuvering the marriage did not take place for six years, until June 11th 1509, seven weeks after the death of Henry's father. Even then it was against the advice of Archbishop Warham, who warned that although Pope Julius had given a dispensation, it was still not legal, in the sight of God, for Henry to marry his brother's widow.

Royal Gossip. As the years went by, royal gossip, which would have caused concern, was rife in the Dunstable inns and alehouses, about the lack of an heir. Their first three royal babies, all sons, had died and then the healthy baby born on February 18, 1516, was a girl; she was baptised Mary. Although two years later Catherine made a pilgrimage to Walsingham there were no more children and Princess Mary's heath was giving cause for concern. A year later Catherine was pregnant again, for the last time, but her daughter was still-born.

At first the relationship between Catherine and Henry appeared unchanged but in 1527 rumours began to spread. Within the year the people of Dunstable must have been aware that Henry was blaming his lack of sons on the fact that he had ignored Archbishop Warham's advice and had married his brother's widow. However, more worldly travellers would

have jeered at these solemn discussions and told the local
people that his majesty had set his lustful eyes on Anne Boleyn
and that she was refusing his advances unless they could be
legally married.

Henry took advantage of the criticism that his marriage was
not strictly legal, to send messengers to the Pope and various
European leaders, asking their 'advice'. During 1532 he heaped
honours and riches on Anne, promised marriage and at last she
gave way; by the end of the year she was pregnant. On 25th
January 1533 they were secretly married[1].

An Annulment at Dunstable. The situation was desperate. The
Pope refused to declare in Henry's favour, but Archbishop
Warham was dead and the new Archbishop, Thomas Cranmer,
was prepared to oblige his king. Dunstable was a suitable place
to decide the King's 'grete and weightie cause' and on the 10th
May 1533 Cranmer rode into the town to meet the Bishops of
London, Winchester and Bath. Together with Prior Markham
and their various advisers, they sat in the Lady Chapel for
nearly two weeks, discussing not only the legality of Henry's
first marriage, but also the advisability and the implication of
standing out against the wishes of their spirtual leader, the
Pope. When on May 23rd, Cranmer wrote to reassure Henry
that they had decided that his marriage to Catherine had never
been legal and had therefore been annulled, Henry was able to
proceed with the coronation.

During the ten days that the discussions were taking place
every bed in Dunstable must have been taken and the inns
packed with gossiping servants and officials connected with the
enquiry and with official and unofficial messengers waiting for
news. When at last the decision was made, the canons, quickly
followed by the burgesses and innkeepers, would have been
the first people in England to know. As they gradually realised
that their popular queen had, after twenty-four years of
marriage, been deposed, the thoughts of many must have

---

1   Antonia Fraser, 'The Six Wives of Henry VIII'.

turned towards Ampthill where the abandoned wife was also waiting for news. To the end of her life she refused to accept the findings of the enquiry. She swore that her marriage to Arthur had never been consummated and so her marriage to Henry was legally binding.

The Church in England

In 1534 an Act of Parliament formalised the break with Rome by declaring Henry to be supreme head of the church. This was followed by a series of changes which converted the church in Dunstable and elsewhere into what may be described as 'Anglo-Catholic'. Teams of civil servants visited the town, obliging each of the canons and all the civil officer to sign that they accepted the Act of Supremacy and Anne as queen. There is no evidence that anyone in this town refused, although at Woburn the abbot, sub-prior and one of the monks were hung for treasons, having refused to conform. This brutal act, so near to Dunstable, may have helped to prevent a revolt here.

The Small Religious Houses are Closed

In 1536 Henry closed the smaller religious houses. It was a popular way of raising money, much of which was supposed to go towards educational projects. If anyone complained, it was pointed out that the small houses had so little income and so few members, that they could not properly carry out their function. Now members would have the opportunity of transferring to a larger, more efficient house. At this stage there was no suggestion that houses such as Dunstable Priory would be asked to close. However, there was soon talk of identifying the inefficient amongst the larger houses and for their leaders to be invited to surrender their houses to the wishes of the King. Inspectors went round making enquiries and writing reports; some of which were true and others not. Bribes were offered and accepted, rumours spread and travellers who asked too many questions were treated with suspicion.

King Henry Stays at The White Horse Inn

In 1508, Henry VII had obtained Ampthill Castle and Great
Park from the third Earl of Kent, of Wrest Park. This became a
very popular hunting lodge for his son, who frequently visited
it at the summer's end, when the plague drove him away from
his London palaces. At different times most of his wives,
children and close companions visited him there, often
breaking their journey in Dunstable and sleeping at the Prior's
house, at the East Street entrance to the Priory.[1]

By 1537 there were strong rumours that Henry intended to
close all the religious houses. The Prior, Gervase Markham,
must have already been feeling anxious before he heard of the
arrangements being made for the King's summer visit. His best
rooms were ready and waiting when he heard that Henry's
steward was in the town, preparing rooms at The White Horse
Inn! He wrote to Archbishop Cranmer begging him to speak to
the King and persuade him to change his mind. If Cranmer
failed to move the King, the Prior hope that Cranmer himself
would use the rooms. Henry eventually stayed at the White
Horse on Thursday 9th and Friday 10th August. He was trying
to avoid confrontation and argument with the Prior about his
plans for the dissolution of the monasteries. Not only was The
White Horse one of the most important inns on the London to
Chester Road but the owner, Thomas Bentley, was one of the
very few property owners who did not pay ground rent to the
Prior[2]. At the back of his inn, near the present New Covenant
Church, he had a bowling green and this was one of Henry's
favourite games. The stone gateway, which still stands in High
Street North, in the late 19th century led to the Anchor pub but
it was originally built as the entrance to The White Horse Inn.

At the time of this visit Jane Seymour was Queen; she did
not accompany Henry because her baby (Edward) was due in
October. Sadly she died twelve days after the birth. Anne of

---

1   For a detailed account of King Henry VIII and Dunstable, see the booklet
     of that name, published in 1991 to mark the 500th Anniversary of King
     Henry's birth.
2   See Chapter 11.

Cleeves, married and divorced in 1540, was followed by Katherine Howard, who married Henry on 28th July 1540. They set out on a leisurely honeymoon, royal progress, arriving in Dunstable about four months before the Priory closed.

Princess Mary Visits Dunstable

Katherine was executed on 13th February 1542 and the following July Henry married for the last time. His bride, the thirty-one year old widow, Catherine Parr, brought Princess Mary, daughter of Catherine of Aragon, back into the family circle and allowed her to join the 'honeymoon' progress, which arrived in Dunstable during September 1543. Included in the princess's expenses are her token payments as she entered the town. The 'King's Boys' (choir boys?) received 7s. 6d. (38p), the King's minstrels, 25s. 0d. (£1.25), the 'Officers at the Threshold' £4 and the 'Guard' who escorted her £4.14s.10d. (£4.74).

Other Royal Visits

On numerous occasions Henry sent the royal children away from London to avoid infection. With their various tutors and their surprisingly large households they must have been well-known in Dunstable as they travelled to and fro to Ampthill or when they were living at nearby Ashridge.

Whether Mary returned to Dunstable when she became Queen, is not recorded. Queen Elizabeth was here when she visited Woburn in 1572. She must also have passed through on her way to Toddington in 1563 and King Edward probably stayed here when he visted Ampthill in 1548.

Chapter 11

The Dissolution of the Monasteries
– 1535 to 1540

In April 1536 there were more than eight hundred religious houses in England and Wales, with nearly ten thousand monks, canons, nuns and friars. Four years later the houses were all closed and their residents had found other homes and often other occupations. The reasons for the dissolution and the fact that this amazing religious and social upheaval went through, in this part of England, with no apparent protest is too complicated a subject to discuss fully here[1].

Briefly Henry VIII was in desperate need of money; the religious houses were extremely wealthy, most of this wealth being in the form of land and property; they were no longer as popular as they had been in previous centuries and in some areas their closure might even have proved to be a popular move. Life at the Priory was no longer as harsh as it had once been, numbers had fallen and members were more often seen out in the local community; it was recorded that they sometimes enjoyed hawking on the Downs or ferreting for rabbits, out at Buckwood (Beechwood–Markyate). Although the Prior had less to do with the running of the town, he still controlled its development. By the 1530s King Henry could probably rely on Dunstablians and others to look at the canons with envy rather than with devout respect. In a very few cases but definitely not in Dunstable, they were no longer living by

---

1   'The Dissolution of the Monasteries', a small book in the Pitkin series, is a brief but comprehensive account. See also J.J.Scarisbrick – 'The Dissolution of the Monasteries – The Case of St. Albans'.

their vows, or carrying out the wishes of their founders.

In the north of England, where the local people did try and prevent the closures, the non-religious part of their protest was based on their concern for accommodation for travellers and their horses, education and employment for their sons and daughters and the care of orphans and sick people. The Dunstablians knew that they already had inns and were no doubt wanting the chance to open more; assuming that they could take over the hospital and school, as the Fraternity had already taken over the almonry,* the people of Dunstable were not so worried about these points as were the people of the more isolated north.†

The Closing of the Dominican Friary

The small religious houses, with an income of less than £200 a year, were closed by Act of Parliament in 1535 but after some discussion the Dominican Friars were excluded. However, as the pressure for voluntary closure grew they surrendered their house in 1538. As they did not receive pensions we cannot trace them, but being educated men they probably found positions as vicars, chaplains or schoolmasters. Their numbers had fallen during the 16th century and they had adapted some of their rooms into a private apartment, which was to be preserved; the rest were to be pulled down. The Bishop of Dover, who rode into Dunstable to supervise the destruction of the church and to make sure the silver plate, the lead from the windows and roof and the bells were safely transported to the Tower of London, wrote to Thomas Cromwell that he had arrived too late. Some had been pledged (in lieu of debts) and the rest was stolen. Thomas Bentley of The White Horse, signed an agreement to rent the site of the late house, the remains of the buildings which the King had ordered to be destroyed, the various orchards and gardens and three cottages on the South Street boundary. The total rent was to be 44s. 8d. (£2.23) per year. His

---

*   There is no recorded proof of this, but it seems likely.

†   In the next book in this series we will find that it was more difficult than they thought.

Foundations of a fireplace uncovered by M.A.S.; a later additon to one of the Friary walls it may have been associated with the 'Marshall's Lodging'. A.J.C.

agreement did not cover the tenant William Marshall's apartments, which included 'one great chamber and two small chambers' in the Great Court[yard] and a stable just inside the main gates. These buildings remained the property of the Crown well into the 19th century and were always described as 'late, Marshall's Lodging'.

Gervase Markham – the Last Prior

Markham became Prior in 1525; he came from a comfortably-off local family and his brother owned property round about. He was the prior when King Henry broke with tradition and stayed at The White Horse Inn. As an educated and intelligent man, used to entertaining visitors from court and parliamentary circles, as they travelled to and from London, he knew all too well what Henry was planning.

The majority of the religious houses were 'surrendered' one by one, at a date chosen by the senior member and his/her advisers, not closed on any set date chosen by the King. Each monk and nun was to be given a pension and the senior member, in this case the Prior, was able to negotiate to improve their financial arrangements. The Augustinian canons were all ordained clergymen and most of them would be able to find livings. Markham made his arrangements carefully and then, like many others, surrendered his house on 31st December 1539.

The Last Canons of Dunstable Priory

For himself, Markham arranged a small house in High Street South and a pension of £60 per year. He lived there for over twenty years, looked after by a housekeeper and housemaid, with a manservant to do the outdoor work. He may have acted as a relief clergyman in and around Dunstable. When he died, in September 1561, Queen Mary's reign and the brief return to Roman Catholicism was over and Queen Elizabeth was on the throne. In his will he left his chalice, vestments and the ornaments which would have been used in a Roman Catholic chapel, to his cousin, ready if ever 'they may at any time hereafter be occupied in the church again'. He was buried on 23rd September 1561, in the surviving part of the Priory Church, over which he had ruled for nearly fifteen years.

The sub-prior, Thomas Claybrooke, received a pension of £9 a year and went to live with the Prior's brother William Markham at his house in Hanbury, Staffordshire. Details concerning the eleven canons can be found as an appendix to 'English Monks and the Suppression of the Monasteries', by G. Baskerville. They received pensions of between £6 and £12 per year.

Just before the Prior surrendered his house he had arranged for his brother, William, and the senior canon's brother, Thomas Kent, of Luton, to receive some of the Priory's property at Pulloxhill and at Husborne Crawley. As a result of this, livings were found for Canon Kent and another canon at these two villages. A third canon became curate at Hockliffe, where the Priory owned a small, roadside hospital. Four others found livings in Buckinghamshire and Hertfordshire and three in Sussex and Surrey. No surviving records have been found concerning the remaining canon, who may have been elderly. After a few years had passed most the the Dunstable canons moved on to better livings and several of them married[1].

A Cathedral for Dunstable?

Changes to the priory buildings came slowly; at first it was hoped that some of them would be saved as part of a great national scheme to break up the over large dioceses. The complete church building nearly became a cathedral with the prior's house becoming a palace for the new bishop and Priory House a hostel for visitors.

At the private archive of Hatfield House is a plan thought to have been drawn up by Lawrence Bradshaw, 1543–44, inscribed 'The Plat [Plan] of Dunstabyll'. It is a ground floor plan of a single-storeyed building listed in the catalogue as a hunting lodge. It was never built but on paper there are no features that would have made it suitable for use as a hunting lodge. There are six suites of rooms each with their own stool room (lavatory) and sharing three chapels; two enclosed courtyards and two enclosed gardens; at the back is an orchard and in the front a larger courtyard; with some small communal rooms in the centre, but no sign of the large dining room and attendant kitchens which one might expect to find if the building was intended to provide accommodation for royal hunting parties[2].

The costing which was prepared for the proposed bishopric

---

1   G. Baskerville. Appendix to English Monks and the Suppression of the Monasteries. Each canon is mentioned by name.

2   R.A.Skelton and J.Summerson prepared the catalogue. A description of Maps and Architectural Drawings at Hatfield House. The Plan is identified as CPM/11/22.

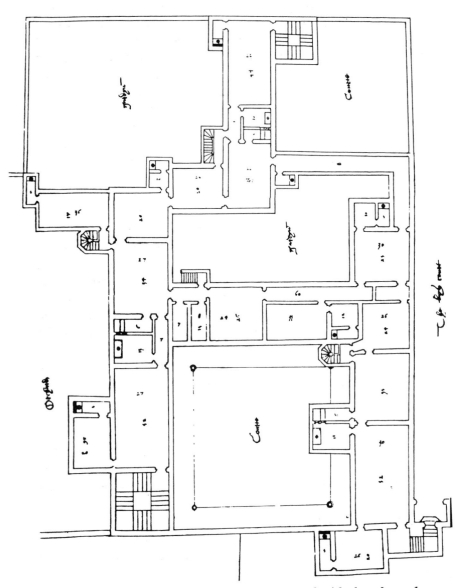

'The Plat of Dunstabyll', a plan possibly connected with the scheme for a cathedral for Dunstable. M.S.

included salaries for a dean, six prebendaries and a reader in divinity[1]. This building may have been intended to replace the residential rooms of the old priory and to provide accommodation for the six prebendaries attached to the new cathedral? Twenty scholars were to be supported at a grammar school in Dunstable and in addition there were to be eight choristers, six 'syngyng men' and 'six peticanons to sing in the quier'. Twenty-three shillings and four pence (£1.17) was estimated as necessary for each boy in the cathedral school and £16. 8s. 4d. (£16.42) for the schoolmaster. Four divinity students were to be supported at Cambridge and two at Oxford; £6. 8s. 4d. (£6.42) was estimated for each of these.

To replace the almshouses which had been provided by the Fraternity, accommodation was to be provided for six 'poore men being old servyng men decayed by Warres or by the Kynges servyce'. The estimate for each of them was the same as for the divinity students and also the 'syngyng men'. As part of the charitable work of the new cathedral £20 was to be set aside as alms for the poor householders of Dunstable. There would still be gates and porter's lodges on both East and South Street, and in return for their £6 per year the porters would also be responsible 'to shave the company'.

Old buildings require constant repairs and £23. 6s. 8d. (£23.33) a year was allowed for this, with a further £20 'to be employed in makying and mendying of high wayes'.

The Buildings Were Taken Down
We do not know how many years went by before the authorities realised that there was no money available for this scheme. The closing of so many religious houses and the confiscation of their land had caused a glut of land on the market. The enormous sums of money collected in the first few years, from many different sources, had been absorbed by the royal and national exchequers. The buildings must be pulled down.

---

1   H.Cole. 'King Henry VIII, Scheme of Bishoprics'.

The Church. The people of Dunstable had supported the west end of the original church for so long that they were awarded this as a parish church, without payment.

Conjectural drawing by Bernard West. A 15th century nave, pulpitum and rood of Dunstable Priory Church. D.T.C.

The Priory Buildings. In 1539–40 officials had supervised the systematic destruction of the religious buildings and the carting away of different types of materials to official collection points. We do not know when those at Dunstable were taken down but undoubtedly local people helped themselves to a great deal of the stone. Some pieces can still be seen which were used for house repairs in West Street and up until a few years ago pieces could be seen in the back walls of Middle Row. When Ellis's, the barber's shop in West Street, was taken down in 1977 the chimney, which had been added to this very old building, had a foundation of carved Totternhoe stone.

Priory House. The future of the Priory was still undecided in 1545 and Richard Greenway was put in charge of the Priory buildings, grounds and 'chief messuage', presumably the Prior's house (soon to be taken down). Nine years later all hopes of the bishopric had slipped away and Richard Denton of the Lyon, in Whites Lane, with some others, bought Priory House. It may have been a clever investment because they soon sold it again and it repeatedly changed hands. The history of this important building will be included in the next volume of this series.

The Town
The Bedfordshire Historical Record Society have published the full rent list of all the ex-religious property which was still in the King's hands in Bedfordshire in 1542. It includes all but a very few pieces in Dunstable which may have already been purchased by the tenants or where wealthy, influential men, like Thomas Bentley, owner of The White Horse, were concerned, may have been put up independently, following the purchase of a licence from the Prior.

The Court of Augmentation
The closing of the monasteries and the acquisition of their property caused a great problem of administration. The crown estates were already getting too big to administer easily so the Court of Augmentation was set up as a central treasury during

the transition and before the reconstitution of the Exchequer. Sir Thomas Pope was the treasurer from 1536 to 1540 and on 28th September 1536, 'Thomas Pope riding with 9 horse to the court about the affairs of the Court of Augmentation, the King's Grace then laying at Dunstable', charges, '6s.8d. per day for the space of three days, that is to say for myne expenses £3. 7s. 8d.' Did they all stay at the White Horse?[1].

The 'Honour of Ampthill'* was formed as a central organising and collecting office for the income from all the religious houses in Bedfordshire. In 1542 Geoffrey Chamber was the 'County Receiver' and the 'Local Receiver' or bailiff was Adam Hilton of the Saracen's Head, who previously had been the Prior's bailiff.

The Rent List of 1542

The publication of these extremely detailed rent lists makes it possible to compare Dunstable as it was when the Priory closed with the much less accurate picture of 1200 (see below). Gone were the wool merchants, the goldsmiths and the Young family. It had become a market town with more emphasis on agriculture but above all it had become, as in the third and fourth centuries AD, dependent on travellers. There were ten inns, three beer houses and a cookhouse mentioned.

Some of the names are recognisable today: the 'Inlands' – to which Englands Lane – Britain Street was once a boundary, other boundaries called Mepes Hedge – now represented by Long Hedge and the 'Road to Leighton' now Leighton Gap, St. Mary's Close up until recently bounded by St. Mary's Street; 'Spondend' which became known as Spoondell, 'Kingsbury Close' behind Kingsbury Court.

The Windmill in **West Street**, referred to in the 13th century, was still there and the lane leading up to it. From these

---

1   Richardson. History of the Court of Augmentations. The quotation is from
    the 8th Report of the Royal Commission of Historic Manuscripts. 1910.
    Ap. Part II.

*   An 'honour' is the name given to an exceptionally large estate made up
    of many separate pieces of land or property.

documents we learn that the Fraternity of St. John the Baptist had their brotherhood house, chaplain's house, four other houses and a smallholding in West Street, and that the church wardens had a house, perhaps an almshouse or workhouse, there. In total, there were twenty-one houses in West Street and two butchers, three smallholdings and the Windmill. At the end of the list, quite unexplained, 'Lady Margaret Hawte 52 shillings and a halfpenny'. Could this be the new owner or tenant of the block of property which Alexander Young gave the Priory?

In **South Street** the market had become known as **Middle Rents**. John Bailey has found sixteenth century timber in several of these remaining buildings[1]. They were built as shops/workshops and each one had three stories with entrances both front and back, (see picture). Nineteen are mentioned, which suggests a block of at least eleven back-to-back units, but several may have already been purchased because the row was probably longer than that. The Tithe Map of 1836 shows eighteen to twenty units.

South Street itself had changed very little from the 13th century. There were still a few big houses and many small ones but several houses had become inns. The Saracen's Head was already there; John Bailey has found sixteenth century timbers in the roof. Adam Hilton the bailiff was paying £4 per year for it. The present building has mainly been rebuilt and includes a second 16th century inn, the "Lower George'. Further along was the New Falcon, tenant Joan England; this may have been the present White Swan. Another inn mentioned was called The Ram and there were beerhouses called the Angel, the Raven and the Owl.

The Friary was let to Thomas Bentley, of the White Horse, except the part previously let to William Marshall which went to Roger Lee. There is mention of the 'great orchard'; could this be connected with the crosses cut in the chalk which were found in the Friary Field?[2]

1   John Bailey, 'Timber Framed Buildings'.
2   Manshead Magazines especially No. 21 and No. 24.

There was a school house in South Street and reference to a common well. The total was 61 houses, 4 inns, 4 beer houses, 3 slaughter-houses, 2 smallholdings and the school. New developments since 1200 were three lanes running from Middle Rents west towards today's Bull Pond Lane. Their possible position was: **Taylor's Lane**, furthest south, through what became Snoxells Farm and is now the carpark beside the Methodist Church, on which was a farm or work yard, a barn and four gardens (one owner being in Middle Rents and three in South Street. **Havewyke Lane**, (recently called Chapel Walk) with one house, one small holding, two barns and two gardens. **Pothyn Lane**, (recently called St. Mary's Lane) which led through a passage in Middle Rents and so into Church Walk. It had six barns (one annexed to a house in West Street) and three gardens.

In **East Street**, (Church Street) the Houghton Chantry had a rent free house for their Chaplain and four other houses. They also had the Swan Inn on the corner of North Street (later known as the Red Lion), with a post across the road to support a sign hanging over the street. There was another inn called the 'Lamme' and a school house which may have been the one attached to the Houghton Chantry.

George Cavendish, friend and biographer of Cardinal Wolsey owned Kingsbury, and may at times have stayed there; it was not included in the rent list. There was a total of 26 houses, 2 inns, 4 smallholdings and a schoolhouse.

In **North Street**, there is evidence of property not included in the King's rent list, e.g. 'Tenement next an inn of the said Thos. [Bentley] called the Whitehorse'. The inn itself is not on the rent list. Another inn occurs in the same way and two houses and a baker's business. One tenement is described as 'containing in itself 6 houses?' Perhaps the site of one of the old 'messuages' (work yards) now developed for housing? There were two mills, one called the 'Glason House'*, 29 houses, 1 shop, 2 inns, 1 forge and 2 smallholdings.

---

*   Later evidence suggests they may have been connected with malting or brewing.

In the middle of the street, equivalent to Middle Rents, was **Whites Lane** which is identified by the Lyon and the Peacock, which stood until 1804 right in the middle of High Street North! Also in the road stood a house called the 'Cokerye' (cookery?). The Lyon was owned by Richard Denton. He died in 1564 and his memorial brass was once in the Priory Church. Total 2 inns and an eating house. The White Hart which stood until 1965 in North Street, was on **Undepelane** (a deep lane?) which ran east and came out near Kingsbury. It had one inn, one house, two granaries, three barns and four gardens.

This gives Dunstable a total of two hundred buildings which were in some way residential. There may be some more independent houses not mentioned and most of the servants' houses which were round courtyards are not mentioned either. The 1671 figure covering all houses was 212 households so by 1542 the town had already taken shape[1].

Sixteenth century shops. The road sign beyond the Midland Bank hides blocks of Totternhoe stone, taken from the Priory, to repair the wall of what became Mr Gutteridge's farm house. This may stand on the site of an even earlier farm house. J.H.

1   B.H.R.S. Vol. XVI.

Chapter 12

The Augustinian Priory –
What We Can See Today

The Great Court [yard]
Standing facing the old gateway which leads into Priory Gardens from the church, the buildings of the canons were all to the east, with the Prior's house and the cellarium (outer parlour and prior's hall and guest chambers) forming the boundary.

To the west of the gate was the 'Great Court of the Canons', a large open space perhaps cobbled and drained, with the barns, cowsheds, pig sties and stables for maybe a hundred horses. There were also bakehouses, brewhouses, and (probably) along Church Walk, small cottages for the lay workers.

The Priory Church of St. Peter
This was originally only part of the whole church, which was the focal part of the life of the Priory. Following the Dissolution, two-thirds of the building was pulled down and the western end which had been used by the people of the town, survived as the parish church. Although more than 450 years have gone by there are still many features in the church to remind us of the early Dunstablians. There is an excellent history display on the north wall.

The Wall at the East End of the church marks the division between what was the parish nave and the canons' quire. The lower part of the wall, with the two blocked archways, is original. On the great church festivals the canons used to

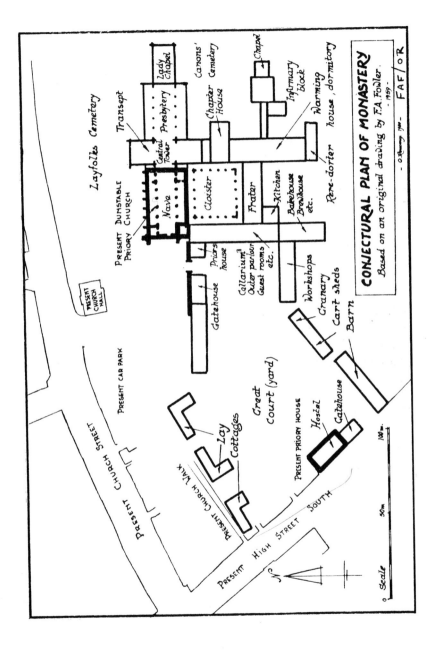

CONJECTURAL PLAN OF MONASTERY

Based on an original drawing by F.A. Fowler

- O Ramsey 1990 - FAF / OR

process down into the nave, through these arches, as part of the celebrations. The two windows and the three statues were a gift to the church in 1962.

The Grave Slab was uncovered in the course of restoration work. It is late 13th century and shows a priest in the clothes of an Augustinian canon. It is made of expensive marble and may have been over the grave of Richard Durrant, son of the Priory benefactor John Durrant. At the time of his death, Richard was resident at the Priory waiting for a living to become vacant.

The Sanctus Bell is on display at the back of the church. Sadly the Annals record nothing about the effect of the 1349 plague, the Black Death, on the people of Dunstable. However, they do record that during the time of the plague the townspeople provided a new bell and called it Mary.

The Marian Pillars, over the vestry door, are a row of ten, carved wooden banisters. The carvings include the royal badges of England and Spain. They date from the reign of Queen Mary and may in some way be connected with the annulment of her mother's marriage.

The St. John the Baptist Chapel was, according to the Priory Annals, consecrated in 1220, in honour of St. John the Baptist. It was for the use of the townspeople, before the whole nave became their parish church. When the burgesses bought a licence, in 1442, to found a religious fraternity, they chose to dedicate it to St. John the Baptist.

The Wooden Carvings, in the roof of the nave, are much older than the present roof (1871). They are thought to date from the 15th century and were preserved when the original, much higher roof, was removed. Omer Roucoux has recently managed to take close-up photographs of these carvings and has been able to prove that they are all slightly different, that they are secular and not religious figures and that just one was once brightly coloured. It is just possible that they represented early members of the Dunstable fraternity.*

---

* For more about these important carvings, see Bedfordshire Magazine, Vol. 24, No. 186, John Lunn, 'Medieval Figures in Dunstable Priory Church'.

*One of a set of wooden carvings from the roof of the Priory Church.
O.R.*

The **Hayward Windows** are one of the modern treasures of the church; those at the west end are known as the 'Priors Window' and the 'Royal Window'. The history of the Priory is recorded in the wonderful colours of modern, stained glass; the number of historical details included is quite amazing.

The **Illustrated Guide** is an excellent example of concise and yet very comprehensive information. If one stands at the east end of the nave and reads the description of the two big windows, all the details become clear.

The **History Corner** is made up a a number of items of historical interest. The large painting is modern. It is an artist's impression of the scene at the Dedication of the Church by Hugh, Bishop of Lincoln, in 1213.

The 'Prior's Window' by John Hayward. A drawing by Andrew Leech, based on a photograph by Omer Roucoux. A.L.

Priory House

Leading from the Great Court (Priory Gardens) out to the left of the gate into South Street, there once stood a porter's lodge and to the right was the hostel for visitors and travellers. The building which stands on the site today, has recently been renovated, but still has walls and pillars which were part of the 13th century hostel. During the renovations a stone fireplace was uncovered, which may have been put in when the building was converted to a private house, some years after the Dissolution.

Kingsbury

Facing the Priory, across East Street, stood the houses, which made up the royal residence, known as Kingsbury. There was probably a large courtyard, similar to the one across the road at the Priory. The palace stood on a nine acre site, opposite the Priory but there is a certain amount of mystery as to its exact position. Excavations by Manshead Archaeological Society, in the gardens of Kingsbury House, before they were used as a site for the flats known as Kingsbury Court, failed to uncover any positive evidence of the old palace. This may be because the gardens were built up over the years, on what had been the courtyard. A Charter issued by King Henry III, in 1227, confirming his father's grant of Kingsbury, to the Priory, included the words – '. . . before the cemetery of the Church of the Blessed Peter towards the north . . .'

About thirty years after the closing of the Priory, the traveller, William Camden, included a very brief history of Dunstable in his book, 'Britannia'[1]. He mentioned that [King Henry I] 'made for him selfe a roiall Manour, or house neere under that place'. [Dunstable]. He also mentions that it was called Kingsbury but does not identify the site. However, William Stukeley, c1723 wrote, 'Kingsbury, the royal seat over – against the church, is now a farm-house'[2]. Finally, G. A. Walpole, who published 'The New British Traveller' in 1784, wrote – 'Dunstable . . . had formerly a royal palace, which was situated opposite the church, some remains of which, still standing, have been repaired, and with some additions converted, into a farm-house called Kingsbury'.

The history of the site after the Dissolution will be included in a later book in this series. In brief, what is now Kingsbury House and the Old Palace Lodge, or a building on their site, became a gentleman's house. The Marsh family, whose descendents founded almshouses and a school in the town, lived there for several generations. By the 19th century it had become a farmhouse and what is now the Norman King was one of the ancient barns. In 1960 contemporary materials were used to convert the barn into a public house.

Underground Passages

(1) The first edition of the Ordinance Survey Map, published in 1880, marked an underground passage from Priory House across to the Priory Church of St. Peter. By the time of the second and subsequent editions they had decided that their information was incorrect and omitted it.* In 1987 Manshead Archaeological Society had the opportunity to test this information. Following the removal of a neglected and unsightly hedge they were allowed to undertake a limited excavation, right across the line where the tunnel would

---

1   First English translation, published in 1610 and quoted by Omer Roucoux in Topic Issue No. 6, 1985.
2   Itinerarium Curiosum, quoted as above.
*   I am grateful to Mr. Barry Horne for this information.

have run. They were able to report that there wasn't and never had been such a passage[1].

(2) There is a legend that there was a passage which ran from Kingsbury, under Church Street and the graveyard, to the Priory Church. This is backed up by the fact that there was what looked like a very small, brick lined tunnel, leading out of the cellar of Kingsbury House, towards the south. However, it was several feet above floor level and was so low that even crawling would have been difficult. Also public service trenches have been dug across the line, on several different occasions and there is no known exit into the vaults of the church.

The Graveyards

In 1970 men digging trenches for gas pipes along the eastern end of the Priory Meadow, discovered the position of the canon's burial ground[2].

The graveyard, which separates the church from the road, was up until the opening of the West Street Cemetery, the town graveyard. This must have continued east, because in 1992 Manshead Archaeological Society uncovered evidence of the graveyard in a Priory Road garden.

The Saracen's Head

This is one of the oldest inns in this district which is still in business. There has been more than one fire and the building has been greatly altered but it stands on the original street level, well below today's road surface. The date when it was first opened as an inn is unknown but at some date before the Dissolution the canons were obliged to provide extra accommodation for travellers. They opened at least two inns along their boundary, The Saracen's Head and the George; the latter became part of the Saracen's.

1 Manshead magazine, Vol. 27 has a full description of the dig and discussion re. this and other underground passages. Vol. 33 covers the various excavations which took place around the area at the Priory 1948–1992.

2 R.Hagen, 1972, 'A Roman Ditch in Dunstable Priory Meadow', Beds. Arch. Journal 7, p.35–38.

Postscript

For some while before it actually happened, the people of Dunstable had had time to get used to the fact that the Priory was about to close. In fact the Prior continued living in the town, while his steward continued to collect their rents and to oversee the market and manor court.

The Honour of Ampthill was rented out by the various kings and queens of England to various of the large land owners of Bedfordshire and they continued to administer the once religious lands on behalf of the Crown. Gradually individual properties were bought privately but much of Dunstable remained Crown property until well into the reign of Queen Victoria.

The Priory had gone but Dunstable still stood on the crossing of two main roads and with the closing of the Priory Hostel there were even greater possibilities for businessmen to invest in the travel and tourist industries.

In the second book of this series, covering the years 1550 to 1850, we will find that North Street was very soon lined with inns and that despite the state of the roads more and more travellers passed through the town. Once again we will find that despite the money that these travellers brought with them they were not all welcome. Soldiers during the 17th century civil war again came to Dunstable stealing food and commandeering horses; the landlord of the Red Lion was killed trying to protect the remaining horses from his stables. Pickpockets, confidence tricksters, horse thieves and highwaymen were regularly arrested in and around the town.

The inn keepers even suspected that they had a witch living amongst them and had her imprisoned at Bedford.

It may be because they lived on the crossing of two main roads and visited inns frequented by the religious and political free thinkers of their day, or maybe it was because their ancestors had developed an independent spirit, struggling against the wishes of the various priors, but we shall find that in the 17th and 18th centuries the people of Dunstable continued to take an active part in many of the national issues of their day.

Using locally grown straw to make baskets, toys and hats must always have been a profitable local hobby but once again it was the presence of the inns and the constant passing of the travellers which caused this to build up first into a cottage industry producing souvenirs and then into a factory-based industry producing bonnets for sale all over the country.

The straw hat factories, the two railways stations, and the further rapid growth of the town will form the background to the third book in this series covering the modern era.

Background Sources

When writing about the history of any Bedfordshire town or village one is extremely grateful for the published research of Miss Joyce Godber, 'The History of Bedfordshire', published by Bedfordshire County Council in 1969, and also to the authors of the 'Victoria County Histories', published between 1904 and 1914. 'Dunstable, its History and Surroundings' by Worthington G. Smith, originally published in 1904, was reprinted by Bedfordshire County Council in 1980. The numerous other published books and articles concerning the medieval history of Dunstable have been listed by Nigel Benson in his 'Dunstable in Detail', published by the Book Castle in 1986. Included in his book are many pictures plus historical details about the old buildings in Dunstable.

Within the text of this book are numerous references to the Manshead Archaeological Society of Dunstable. In addition to their book 'Ancient Dunstable', originally written by C.L. (Les) Matthews, then revised and enlarged by Joan Schneider and re-published in 1989, their annual journals contain descriptions of the many 'digs' they have carried out, in and around the town.

In the first volume of the 'Bedfordshire Magazine', 1947/48, there were articles about the Priory Church, the Fraternity of St. John the Baptist and other subjects; since then there have been useful and varied articles in every volume. These can be traced in the first twenty volumes by using the Index, produced by Yvonne Nicholls and published in 1987.

Of the three records written at the Priory, the 'Annales Prioratus de Dunstapilia' was published in Latin as part of the Rolls Series, 1866, but the other two, the 'Charters' and the 'Tractatus, or Treatise' were both published by the Bedfordshire Historical Record Society. The former is volume 10, 1926, and the latter, volume 19, 1937. The Court of Augmentation Accounts for Bedfordshire made up volumes 63 and 64, 1984/85, both edited by Yvonne Nicholls.

INDEXES

General

A

Alan the goldsmith, 36
Ampthill, 87, 92, 93, 94, 104, 105, 115
Angerus, House of, 38
Anne Boleyn, Queen, 90, 91, 92
Anne of Cleeves, Queen, 93, 94
Anjou, Count of, 14, 74
Arthur, (brother of Henry VIII), 90, 92
Ashridge Forest, 33
Ashridge House, 94

B

Ball, John, 73
Barnet (Herts.), 71
Barnwell Priory (Cambs.), 20
Barrett, Dora, 77, 78
Bateman, William, 73
Battle, John of, 76
Battlesden, 31
Beauchamp, William de, 50, 54, 57, 61
Bedford, 4, 6, 42, 50, 51, 52, 53, 54, 56, 57, 58, 61, 65, 66, 116
Belvoir Castle, (Lincs.), 36
Bentley, Thomas, 93, 96, 103, 105, 106
Berkhamstead, (Herts.), 3, 4, 14, 33, 55, 78
Black Death, 30, 110
Blunde, Thomas and Justine, 46
Boarscroft, (Herts.), 3
Bradbourne (Derby.), 39
Bradshaw, Lawrence, 99
Braybrook, Christiana de, 57
Braybrook, Henry de, 56, 57, 59, 60
Breauté, Falkes, Margaret, wife of, 50, 51, 60

Breauté, Falkes de, 50, 51, 52, 53, 54, 56, 57, 58, 59, 61
Breauté, William de, 56, 58
British Museum, 29, 31, 82, 83, 84
Buckwood, Beechwood (Herts.), 2, 28, 31, 32, 95
Bunyan, Ralph, 39
Bury St. Edmunds, (Suf.), 71

C

Caddington, 1, 2, 3, 4, 11, 43, 63, 86
Calcutt, Houghton Regis, 28
Cambridge, 22, 101
Canterbury, Archbishops of, 16, 58, 90, 91, 93
Cantilupe, Millicent de, 53
Cantilupe, William de, 53, 57, 70
Canute, King, 1
Catherine, of Aragon, Queen, 86, 87, 89, 90, 92, 94
Catherine Parr, Queen, 94
Cauldwell Priory, 61
Cavendish, George, 106
Chadde, Henry, 16
Chalgrave, 28, 29, 43, 79
Chamber, Geoffrey, 104
Chantry of Houghton Regis, 106
Chaucer, Geoffrey, 104
Cherry, John, M.A., 83, 84
Cistercians, 26, 43
Clithero, Rev. J., 31
Colchester, 9
Corfe Castle, (Dorset), 58
Cous, Adamle, 43
Cranmer, Thomas, 91, 93
Cromwell, Thomas, 96
Croyser, William, 73
Cuthwulf, 1

Dunstable Priory

Dunstable Town

Books Published by THE BOOK CASTLE

JOURNEYS INTO HERTFORDSHIRE: Anthony Mackay.
Foreword by The Marquess of Salisbury, Hatfield House. Nearly 200 superbly detailed ink drawings depict the towns, buildings and landscape of this still predominantly rural county.

JOURNEYS INTO BEDFORDSHIRE: Anthony Mackay.
Foreword by The Marquess of Tavistock, Woburn Abbey. A lavish book of over 150 evocative ink drawings.

ARCHAEOLOGY OF THE CHILTERNS: edited by Robin Holgate.
The latest research by authoritative experts throughout the area.

NORTH CHILTERNS CAMERA, 1863–1954: From the Thurston Collection in Luton Museum: edited by Stephen Bunker.
Rural landscapes, town views, studio pictures and unique royal portraits by the area's leading early photographer.

LEAFING THROUGH LITERATURE: Writers' Lives in Hertfordshire and Bedfordshire: David Carroll.
Illustrated short biographies of many famous authors and their connections with these counties.

THROUGH VISITORS' EYES: A Bedfordshire Anthology:
edited by Simon Houfe.
Impressions of the county by famous visitors over the last four centuries, thematically arranged and illustrated with line drawings.

THE HILL OF THE MARTYR: An Architectural History of St. Albans Abbey: Eileen Roberts.
Scholarly and readable chronological narrative history of Hertfordshire and Bedfordshire's famous cathedral. Fully illustrated with photographs and plans.

LOCAL WALKS: South Bedfordshire and North Chilterns:
Vaughan Basham. Twenty-seven thematic circular walks.

LOCAL WALKS: North and Mid-Bedfordshire:
Vaughan Basham. Twenty-five thematic circular walks.

CHILTERN WALKS: Hertfordshire, Bedfordshire and North Buckinghamshire: Nick Moon.
Part of the trilogy of circular walks, in association with the Chiltern Society. Each volume contains thirty circular walks.

CHILTERN WALKS: Buckinghamshire: Nick Moon.

CHILTERN WALKS: Oxfordshire and West Buckinghamshire:
Nick Moon.

OXFORDSHIRE WALKS: Oxford, the Cotswolds and the Cherwell Valley: Nick Moon.
One of two volumes planned to complement Chiltern Walks: Oxfordshire and complete coverage of the county, in association with the Oxford Fieldpaths Society.

FOLK: Characters and Events in the History of Bedfordshire and Northamptonshire: Vivienne Evans.
Anthology about people of yesteryear – arranged alphabetically by village or town.

LEGACIES: Tales and Legends of Luton and the North Chilterns: Vic Lea. Twenty-five mysteries and stories based on fact, including Luton Town Football Club. Many photographs.

ECHOES: Tales And Legends of Bedfordshire and Hertfordshire Vic Lea. Thirty, compulsively retold historical incidents.

ECCENTRICS and VILLAINS, HAUNTINGS and HEROES. Tales from Four Shires: Northants., Beds., Bucks. and Herts.: John Houghton. True incidents and curious events covering one thousand years.

THE RAILWAY AGE IN BEDFORDSHIRE: Fred Cockman. Classic, illustrated account of early railway history.

BEDFORDSHIRE'S YESTERYEARS Vol. 1: The Family, Childhood and Schooldays: Brenda Fraser-Newstead. Unusual early 20th century reminiscences, with private photographs.

BEDFORDSHIRE'S YESTERYEARS Vol 2: The Rural Scene: Brenda Fraser-Newstead. Vivid first-hand accounts of country life 2 or 3 generations ago.

WHIPSNADE WILD ANIMAL PARK: 'MY AFRICA': Lucy Pendar. Foreword by Andrew Forbes. Introduction by Gerald Durrell. Inside story of sixty years of the Park's animals and people – full of anecdotes, photographs and drawings.

FARM OF MY CHILDHOOD, 1925–1947: Mary Roberts. An almost vanished lifestyle on a remote farm near Flitwick.

DUNSTABLE WITH THE PRIORY, 1100–1550: Vivienne Evans. Dramatic growth of Henry I's important new town around a major crossroads.

DUNSTABLE DECADE: THE EIGHTIES: – A Collection of Photographs: Pat Lovering. A souvenir book of nearly 300 pictures of people and events in the 1980s.

DUNSTABLE IN DETAIL: Nigel Benson. A hundred of the town's buildings and features, plus town trail map.

OLD DUNSTABLE: Bill Twaddle. A new edition of this collection of early photographs.

BOURNE AND BRED: A Dunstable Boyhood Between the Wars: Colin Bourne. An elegantly written, well-illustrated book capturing the spirit of the town over fifty years ago.

ROYAL HOUGHTON: Pat Lovering. Illustrated history of Houghton Regis from the earliest times to the present.

THE CHANGING FACE OF LUTON: An Illustrated History:
Stephen Bunker, Robin Holgate and Marian Nichols.
Luton's development from earliest times to the present busy industrial town. Illustrated in colour and monochrome. The three authors from Luton Museum are all experts in local history, archaeology, crafts and social history.

THE MEN WHO WORE STRAW HELMETS: Policing Luton, 1840–1974: Tom Madigan.
Meticulously chronicled history; dozens of rare photographs; author served Luton Police for nearly fifty years.

BETWEEN THE HILLS: The Story of Lilley, a Chiltern Village:
Roy Pinnock.
A priceless piece of our heritage – the rural beauty remains but the customs and way of life described here have largely disappeared.

EVA'S STORY: Chesham Since the Turn of the Century: Eva Rance
The ever-changing twentieth-century, especially the early years at her parents' general stores, Tebby's, in the High Street.

THE TALL HITCHIN SERGEANT: A Victorian Crime Novel based on fact: Edgar Newman.
Mixes real police officers and authentic background with an exciting storyline.

COUNTRY AIR: SUMMER and AUTUMN: Ron Wilson.
The Radio Northampton presenter looks month by month at the countryside's wildlife, customs and lore.

COUNTRY AIR: WINTER and SPRING: Ron Wilson.
This companion volume completes the year in the countryside.

Specially for Children

VILLA BELOW THE KNOLLS: A Story of Roman Britain:
Michael Dundrow. An exciting adventure for young John in Totternhoe and Dunstable two thousand years ago.

ADVENTURE ON THE KNOLLS: A Story of Iron Age Britain:
Michael Dundrow. Excitement on Totternhoe Knolls as ten-year-old John finds himself back in those dangerous times, confronting Julius Caesar and his army.

THE RAVENS: One Boy Against the Might of Rome: James Dyer.
On the Barton Hills and in the south-each of England as the men of the great fort of Ravensburgh (near Hexton) confront the invaders.

Further titles are in preparation.
All the above are available via any bookshop, or from the publisher and bookseller

THE BOOK CASTLE
12 Church Street, Dunstable, Bedfordshire, LU5 4RU
Tel: (0582) 605670

215